The Soulful Cottage

The Soulful Cottage

CREATING A CHARMING AND PERSONAL HOME

FIFI O'NEILL

With photography by
MARK LOHMAN

CICO BOOKS
LONDON NEW YORK

Senior designer Toni Kay
Editor Sophie Devlin
Production manager Gordana Simakovic
Senior commissioning editor Annabel Morgan
Art director Sally Powell
Creative director Leslie Harrington

Published in 2024 by Ryland Peters & Small
20–21 Jockey's Fields
London WC1R 4BW
and
341 East 116th Street
New York, NY 10029

www.rylandpeters.com

Text copyright © Fifi O'Neill 2024
Design copyright © CICO Books 2024
Photography by Mark Lohman
Additional photography by Edmund Barr,
    John Ellis and Andrea Pietrangeli
For photography credits and copyright
information, see page 186.

10 9 8 7 6 5 4 3 2 1

ISBN 978-1-80065-382-5

A CIP record for this book is available
from the British Library.

Library of Congress CIP data
has been applied for.

Printed and bound in China

Contents

Introduction

"Decoration is really about creating a quality of life, and a beauty in that life that nourishes the soul, that makes life beautiful."

Albert Hadley

SOULFUL COTTAGES have their very own evocative characteristics, each chosen for its emotional connection to the things that matter most in your life.

It's not about following design rules but about imbuing your home with comfort, inspiration, joy and, ultimately, a sense of belonging. From unique architectural features to furnishings, meaningful displays, heirlooms, fabrics, palettes and more, all facets of a soulful home have a deep meaning that resonates with your inner self.

Surrounding yourself with deeply personal items heightens the senses and creates a visual journal that communicates the soul to a room. Whatever their provenance, from family heirlooms to newly acquired pieces, their worth is sentimental rather than monetary. It stems from a personal relationship.

These decorative choices often elicit memories and milestones of our lives. Lightly blemished and gently peeling wood, painted surfaces and patinated metals lend an air of history and stability, while texture and tone contribute a sense of place for a truly timeless look.

When all the elements come together to tell your unique story, they encourage a sense of harmony, permanence, intentionality and humanity. In turn, these qualities establish the aura that is the very essence of a soulful interior.

THE
ELEMENTS

LEFT In this bedroom, original arched doors opening onto a wraparound porch emphasize the home's 19th-century architecture. Painted weathered vintage flooring and a curvy iron table also showcase elements of the building's history. A lush fern is evocative of the era.

OPPOSITE ABOVE Whitewashed and distressed doors and walls have a timeless feel, especially when enhanced with a hand-painted motif and fitted with authentic hardware.

OPPOSITE CENTER Simple but shapely clear vases hold frilly stems of Queen Anne's lace/cow parsley and blowsy peonies that let the texture and faded layers of paint of rustic wallboards take center stage.

OPPOSITE BELOW Black iron garden lanterns on graceful brackets provide a sculptural element against a simple white backdrop.

Unique Features

Soulful cottages are usually (but not always) older than those built in recent years, which means they often come with architectural character that conveys a sense of history. Many of the homes featured in this book have one-of-a-kind features that their owners have embraced for their period charm.

Wainscoting, beams, planks, beadboard, fireplaces, arched doorways, transom windows, moldings and carvings have long been integral components of the traditional cottage. These attributes honor an era when quality craftsmanship and attention to detail were highly valued. They instantly instill a sense of home, permanence and a timeless aesthetic.

But not all unique features come from original architecture. Weathered and painted woods sporting their original patina or layers of color and period hardware—such as doorknobs, hinges, handles and more—also contribute to the look and feel of a specific time, as do honest, natural materials: salvaged woods, worn stones, exposed bricks and aged metals. Repurposing and recycling items made from existing materials is high on the must-have list. Lighting plays a role, too, from chandeliers to lanterns and sconces that showcase the charm and nostalgia associated with earlier times.

The confluence of original architectural features, unique details and items with a deep personal connection celebrates individual interpretation, exudes warmth and livability and contributes to the longevity, enrichment and allure of soulful cottage interiors.

ABOVE This bed was built from old planks with a headboard fashioned from bleached wood and a salvaged garden gate. Even the pillows were sewn from vintage fabric. The disparate materials are united by their organic textures that create layers of intrigue and interest.

FAR LEFT Affixed to a headboard made of leftover fence wood, a shelf bracket holds a vintage-style light bulb with simply wrapped cord for a rustic look.

LEFT A wired antique birdcage becomes a one-of-a-kind light fixture that together with a vintage mirror bring charming touches to a small bathroom.

The rugged finish of a perfectly weathered barn door and the glittery, delicate crystals of a vintage chandelier add texture and authenticity to a neutral corner. The shapely lamp, linear mirror and modern sofa provide a sleek contrast. A woolly faux-fur pillow balances the smoother, more sophisticated fabrics.

OPPOSITE Each piece of furniture inherited from the previous generation has special stories attached to it. A childhood bed and dresser/chest of drawers, whether or not a matching set, often hold precious memories because of the early years they evoke.

ABOVE Even if their background is unknown, found and forgotten salvaged pieces like this vintage chair can become storytellers. Reimagined in white, it whispers a new tale, one of artistic visions and second chances.

Favorite Furniture

Though they might express varied styles—rustic, country, coastal, vintage or romantic—soulful cottages share an affinity for a homey, warm and personable aesthetic. And nothing illustrates their singular identity more than the furnishings that give each one its authentically warm and welcoming environment.

The options for cottage furniture are limitless, as long as they result in interiors that feel inviting. The look isn't rooted in any specific era. Instead, it places an emphasis on creating a unique home with rooms that are layered with well-loved pieces and comfortable materials. Mixing new and old, found and bought, vintage and handmade creates a lived-in vibe. Furniture with weathered or distressed patinas brings texture and interest to spaces and helps to tell a story. It's all about real-life homes brimming with personality, exuding joy and keeping us connected to what truly matters: family, home and heritage.

Varying silhouettes and layering the materials, colors, patterns and textures of upholstered pieces also establish depth and contrast. Reborn with cotton slipcovers, sink-in sofas and cushy armchairs honor the stories of families past. Refinished and painted, old garden chairs take on a new look and a new function, while vintage shutters act as closet doors and a salvaged farm table paired with refurbished cane chairs becomes a dining-room focal point.

Passed on from one generation to the next, inherited pieces and found items are especially precious because of the priceless memories they hold that instantly bond us to our homes.

LEFT This tiny seaside cottage has kept its original exterior, but on the inside it has welcomed fresh, simple and contemporary furniture that honors its roots and its history.

ABOVE A curated selection of honest, organic materials, rich textures and cohesive hues surrounds the cozy sofa, which is hugged by a marble-topped side table. The soothing neutral tones in this corner underscore the modern aesthetic.

OPPOSITE Acquired from different sources but united by their era, a circa 1930s dresser/chest of drawers and mirror, both still with their original paint, turned out to be a perfect match.

Meaningful Art

Our homes are our refuges, places where we can rest, but they should also reflect who we are. The artworks with which we decorate our spaces are one of the distinguishing aspects that most clearly express our individuality.

When a piece of art resonates with you, it creates an emotional framework for your soulful space. It's a way to uplift your mood, create calm and serenity and evoke something personal that nothing else can. It not only expresses feelings and thoughts but also has the ability to create a connection between us and like-minded others with whom we share emotions.

Whether you collect paintings, sculptures, photographs or even old books, the deeper meaning of art is the feelings, thoughts and ideas it communicates.

Colors, shapes, symbolic objects and cultural references also imbue art with layers of interpretation that may be different for each person. Vintage works acquire layers of meaning and authenticity over time.

However you choose to display art—from walls to bookshelves, tables or windowsills—try to vary sizes and shapes, giving each artwork its own place in your home. It's those subtle touches that provide and enhance the connection between you and your surroundings and bring a true sense of home to a space.

OPPOSITE Reminiscent of a time when black-and-white or sepia-toned images were more prevalent, vintage photographs of family and friends communicate personal emotions and elicit feelings of nostalgia. This example is preserved behind clear Plexiglass.

RIGHT United by a monochromatic palette but singular in texture and shape, a grouping of small antiques exemplifies the visually intriguing impact of pieces that hold a connection with the past.

ABOVE Based on 17th-century carvings by European priests, santos cage dolls confer a sacred aura to a home.

Paris Haute Couture

OPPOSITE Displayed against a soft-hued backdrop, a collection of figurative paintings titled *Poetic Portraits* evokes a peaceful time conducive to gentle memories.

ABOVE Handmade by the owner's friend, this dream catcher wall hanging has symbolic embellishments such as feathers and beads. It holds sentimental value by honoring the connection between giver and receiver.

RIGHT A Californian landscape oil painting nods to the inhabitants' home state. The antique washstand below makes a tasteful perch for an ironstone platter with a medicine bottle displaying freshly cut blooms.

LEFT Infused with reverence for the past, these jeweled creations—necklaces, rosaries, earrings and more—have been crafted using pieces from broken or discarded items. They hold countless stories within their vintage beads, sparkling rhinestones and calm turquoises.

OPPOSITE ABOVE When scraps of vintage fabric are brought together to create a new belt or a bag, that item becomes the keeper of memories.

OPPOSITE CENTER Dainty tea sets are always charming. Though they carry the distinction of having graced tables for decades, their true value is that they once belonged to our grandmothers.

OPPOSITE BELOW Whatever their material, finish or function, heart-shaped objects like these candlesticks carry the most meaningful sentiment: love.

Heirloom Objects

An heirloom is typically defined as a valuable object that has belonged to a family for several generations, but these treasures can come in all shapes, forms and styles. They are essentially pieces that have withstood the test of time and trends. Heirlooms may also have a specific connection to a person or a different time.

Cost does not determine the value of heirlooms. What counts is their history and sentimental meaning, as well as their craftsmanship, which is often of a quality not found in contemporary pieces.

A true heirloom is something that was built to last, ensuring it would be passed on from generation to generation. Books were leather-bounded, jewelry showcased rare stones and intricate fittings and clothes were well tailored using fine fabrics. The list goes on to include fine art, old photographs, letters, journals, vintage textiles, collected trinkets, china, silverware and more.

The interesting thing about heirlooms is that they can be set aside for many years before being rediscovered and finding a new purpose. Handmade items are even more special because of the time and effort that went into making them, and how they can be recast—for instance, think of reupholstering an old sofa or chair or piecing together broken parts of disparate jewelry into a new necklace or bracelet.

The true worth of heirlooms lies in their past. When an item is imbued with its original owner's story, memory or personality, it transcends from something of monetary value to a truly priceless and irreplaceable object.

20 SEPT 1997
RAINBOW FALLS
VIA SEASIDE
JAMMIN' JAVA
THE MERC
VIA IRELAND
MODESTO 2000
AIDAN 10·4·00
PASADENA 2001
2001 FRANKLIN
McCREARY'S PUB
LIAM 8·19·02
2005 _____ILL
FINN 7·2__
10 YEARS 20__

OPPOSITE Artwork doesn't have to be a fine painting or sculpture. Here, framed with wood salvaged from a family's barn, a custom subway scroll lists their special dates and memorable places.

ABOVE Handmade gifts from friends are especially sentimental. This cross and photo frame have been artistically and painstakingly embellished with vintage rhinestones and other adornments.

RIGHT Grouping items from various eras and materials weaves together a unique story. This nostalgic tableau of faded glamour creates a link between past and present.

Timeless Layers

The most inviting rooms show the right balance of textural elements through furnishings, objects, materials, finishes, fabrics and colors. Layering pulls together these individual elements to form a cohesive overall look that makes a room feel uniquely personal and inviting. Simply put, layers are decorating gold.

One of the easiest ways to create gorgeous layers is to devise vignettes: little stories that you tell with decor. And in a soulful cottage, the best vignettes are those that speak of you.

The layering concept can easily accommodate contrasting textures and finishes, the rough with the smooth, as long as they are thoughtfully balanced with one another. Distressed, worn or painted furniture and fixtures always appear to be made for each other and promote a sense of home and familiarity. The goal is to create a tactile experience with many points of interest that offer visual weight and rhythm.

Soft furnishings with knitted, braided or woven materials can be subtle, yet the sum of their parts is beautifully synergistic. When mixed judiciously, cozy and easygoing textiles such as wool, cotton and linen work together with more delicate ones like lace and silk to make something magical.

The layered decorating philosophy also doesn't discriminate against patterns and colors. Instead, it takes a playful approach to both. Uplifting hues and homey prints featuring gingham, florals and ticking stripes are a wonderful way to create a cocooning effect in your soulful cottage.

OPPOSITE ABOVE
Textured surfaces showing period stenciling and years of wear contribute complexity, interest and tactility to a vintage dining table. Striped linens add a subtle touch of color.

OPPOSITE CENTER
To create layers on newly painted wood, apply a bit of dark wax to the corners and edges of a piece and gently rub away the excess for an aged effect.

OPPOSITE BELOW
Enamel pots, kettles, baking pans and more have been around since the 1800s. They offer a multitude of patterns, including the mottled design seen on this vintage pitcher/jug.

RIGHT With pleasing contrasts of color, pattern, texture and shape, the decorative elements in this room play off one another to achieve a cohesive whole. The many layers add visual intrigue and feel effortless.

ABOVE In a cottage interior, the goal is to compose an overall visual harmony between original features and decorative accents to convey a lived-in aesthetic and a unique atmosphere.

OPPOSITE Whether furniture, lighting, architectural fragments or garden goods, salvaged remnants instantly layer a space with history and meaning. Their mismatched charm creates a look that is as characterful as it is personal.

Against neutral walls, the gentle play of soft hues and deeper undertones from the colorful application of floral patterns cultivates a fresh and subtle vibe. The overall effect in this room is evocative of a cottage garden.

Pretty Palettes

The transformative power of color is unparalleled, and when it comes to soulful spaces, soft and undeniably pretty watercolor shades are favored for their soothing and tranquil ambiance. By their very nature, these hues' gentle and muted demeanor makes them the mainstay of cottage style.

Pastels and neutrals have a calming influence that promotes peace of mind, ideal for the soulful cottage aesthetic. Imagine faded blues, sun-bleached greens, barely-there pinks, creamy yellows and hushed grays.

When devising a pretty palette for your home, a natural place to start is the color of the walls. However, to be effective, your scheme has to look beyond the paint or wallpaper and incorporate other elements, too—from furniture to textiles, artworks and other decorative accessories.

Soft-toned furnishings accentuated with pillows and blankets make for a cohesive whole that adds to the sense of quiet comfort and inviting atmosphere, while fabrics such velvet, chenille or faux fur contribute a subtle touch of luxury. Art and accessories within the same color family bring yet more interest to the harmonious visual narrative.

Always remember that there is no "one size fits all" rule. When leaning into vibrant hues or richer tones, the more dominant colors are often tempered by quieter ones that bring balance to the mix. The palette you choose is a canvas for personal expression. But unlike words, it tells your story in hues and shades. In the end, the right palette is the one that says "home" to you.

PAGE 31 ABOVE Anything can inspire a color scheme. For this tiny cottage exterior, the paint color was based on a delicate pink blouse. A white trim complements the sweet shade, while natural wood keeps it grounded.

PAGE 31 BELOW The subtle rose-and-gray theme of a wall mural forms the basis for a romantic pink-and-white bedroom with pillows and throws in the same color family.

OPPOSITE LEFT Soft, rosy hues get a lift when accompanied by deeper ones and balanced with soothing shades of blue and green. It's a fresh palette that recalls the outdoors.

OPPOSITE ABOVE RIGHT This little girl's bedroom favors a quiet, feminine palette of pretty pastels, with pink and cream highlighted as her particular favorites.

OPPOSITE BELOW RIGHT Inspired by the ocean's shades and seashells, this beachside tablescape has a calming, green-tinted palette of sea-washed, silvery blues, aqua, teal and pearlescent whites.

RIGHT Inside the same property, the interplay of light, color and texture orchestrates a harmonious palette of neutrals and blues to create an inviting space that whispers of tranquility. Natural elements highlight the beauty of beach finds and organic materials.

Finding Your Style

There are many comforting aspects of soulful interiors and one of the most endearing is how many style options they offer, regardless of whether your home is old or new. These one-of-a-kind homes do not follow specific rules, but rather each reflects its inhabitants' particular preferences and life stories.

Whether you favor a rustic vernacular, 1970s retro, the unpretentious coziness of shabby style, the nostalgic appeal of vintage or an organic, contemporary look, soulful interiors have an individual and highly personal feel that is unique because it's defined by your passions and draws on memories and connections that enrich your life.

Authenticity and intentionality are two of the elements that make your style your own. The diverse interiors in this book showcase a variety of family heirlooms, rescued finds and artisanal goods, not just in older homes but also in many newer or refurbished ones whose owners subscribe to the soulful decorating philosophy.

Color schemes, collections, souvenirs, art, furnishings, cultural influences or time periods, anything is fair game as long as the items you choose resonate with your emotions through their significance or legacy. It's an approach that transcends aesthetics.

Perfection is not the goal; it's all about how your decor supports and uplifts you, and fosters an inner harmony between you and your space. Simply put, when your home makes you feel happy, comfortable, connected and at peace, you have found your style.

ABOVE The materials, muted colors, slightly distressed finishes and decorative items in this kitchen denote an affinity with the unpretentious country farmhouse style. A monochromatic color palette is at its core. The aesthetic is beloved for its approachable and comforting vibes.

OPPOSITE Cheerful colors, bold patterns and fanciful accessories come together in this charming, whimsical interior. Though the look is uplifting and quirky, it's not chaotic—there is a sense of harmony in the use of color and composition.

OPPOSITE & LEFT When salvage meets femininity, decor takes on an unequivocally bohemian, romantic aura. Rescued furnishings, mismatched textiles, raw materials and exotic lighting manage to feel cohesive despite their diverse origins and create a free-spirited atmosphere.

ABOVE & RIGHT Pared-down furnishings and curated accessories make for an uncluttered interior, but here the look still has plenty of charm. The simple shapes and organic materials of essential items are a minimalist's dream of living a meaningful life with less.

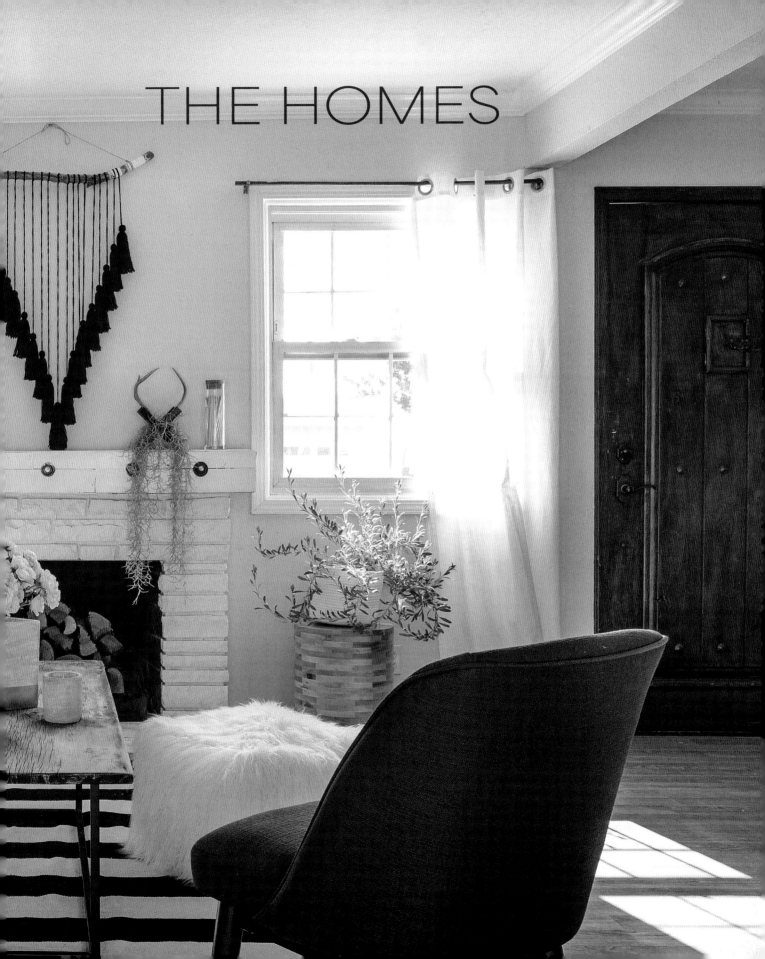

THE HOMES

Rooted in Time

OPPOSITE The couple painted and distressed the oak table, which had been left in the garage by the previous owners. The armoire was a bargain find from a local antiques store. A mix of gingham and floral fabrics instills a lighthearted appeal.

RIGHT Glorious roses draped over an arbor invitingly frame the entrance to Daniel and Louise's home. The colorful blooms add to the allure of a brick pathway and Gothic-style picket fence while contributing undeniable charm and curb appeal to this quaint cottage.

Room to Grow

The year was 1992 and garden designer Louise O'Brien-Schridde had been looking at property after property. She hoped to find a place that would remind her husband Daniel Schridde of his childhood home, a beautiful 1918 farmhouse on Wing Lake in Bloomfield Hills, Michigan. Her real estate agent called to tell her about a property that would soon be on the market: an interesting Spanish Revival dwelling in Burbank, California next to a country cottage. "I told him I wanted to see the gingerbread house and not the Spanish one," Louise recalls. She got the address and went to take a look.

> "The best rooms have something to say about the people who live in them."

David Hicks

EVEN FROM THE OUTSIDE, it was clear that the home needed a lot of work, but Louise fell in love instantly. "The realtor mentioned that he knew the family and if we made an offer they might be willing to sell." So the couple did just that, and a deal was struck—without them ever having seen the inside. "We were not allowed into the house until the closing date, but I couldn't wait," says Louise. "So one day, my sister and I climbed through a window while the owner was out."

The old core of the house was built in 1923 around a tiny galley kitchen; the den had been added in 1941, but the windows had never been installed. Other quirks included a 60-square-foot/5.6-square-meter bathroom with three internal walls. "Though the layout was odd, and the property was a complete fixer-upper, it was quaint and cozy with many small rooms reminiscent of a rabbit warren," Louise recalls. "On the plus side, the former owner had built the house with attention to detail, including mahogany windows, trim and cabinets, a beautiful rock fireplace and oak floors throughout."

If there ever was a creative duo, it has to be Louise and Daniel, who share their passion and knowledge for beautiful landscapes through their company O'Brien Schridde Designs. The dynamic couple turned their artistic hands to their home with the same love and passion they bestow on all their projects. Nothing could curb their enthusiasm and soon the renovations were underway, including the addition of 1,300 square feet/120 square meters to the original footprint.

"Our objective was to expand the home but retain the look and feel of a small cottage, so the new space was blended into the original design," Daniel explains. "We relocated the staircase, tore down almost all the interior walls and added a master suite and a farmhouse-style kitchen large enough to entertain our family and friends." The couple did most of the work themselves—from taking walls down to installing ceilings and sanding floors by hand. And once all the construction was complete, they set out to personalize their new home.

"Daniel and I both love old things because they have a past. They define our place in history," says Louise. "There is something special about loving an item that has been loved by so many before you."

PAGES 44–45 & OPPOSITE A view of the garden from every window and ample space for entertaining were top priorities when adding onto the original kitchen. Daniel took care of the construction while Louise stained, painted and distressed every surface and, with a friend, hung wallpaper from Calico. Above the pantry, a niche keeps cookbooks within reach. Cabinet doors conceal a collection of vases used daily for fresh flowers.

"There is something special about loving an item that has been loved by so many before you."

It's a philosophy that she and Daniel have instilled in their now grown-up sons Max and Miles. "Our home is a hodgepodge of hand-me-downs, worn and weathered found items and pieces we made ourselves. Regardless of their financial value, family heirlooms are priceless," she continues. A case in point is the many cherished treasures from Daniel's mother Jutta's home in Germany. "She has impeccable eclectic country taste," Louise notes. "Together with the many country magazines we collected, Jutta was very instrumental in inspiring our cozy, inviting and comfortable aesthetic."

Among the many elements that define the Schriddes' style, texture makes the top of the list. The walls of their home are paneled, painted, papered, stenciled and distressed, and the floors show off hand-painted patterns and colors. Window treatments and upholstery add another layer of tactile charm.

LEFT "So many of the items in the living room represent our family history," Louise explains. "When Daniel's mother sold her home, she gave us a number of pieces, including the coffee table, the oar, the chandelier and the painting of the tree, which was done by Daniel's grandfather."

The garden also needed attention. "All the plants were dead and so was the lawn. As for the trees, they looked pitiful," Louise explains. She and Daniel brought their landscape design skills to the project, with impressive results. "We built a picket fence out front, added arbors and then started planting our beautiful roses, trees and shrubs." They also laid out brick patios and walkways.

"Curb appeal sets the mood—when someone is walking by, oftentimes we see them smile when they pause to look at our home and garden," Daniel says. "It lets us know they are getting what our home is all about: considerate, comfy and welcoming."

It has been a little over 30 years since Louise and Daniel first set foot in the house that now holds many cherished memories. It has doubled in size, risen from the 1994 earthquake and been filled with country charm inside and out. "It has truly been a labor of love," says Louise. "But ultimately, what makes a home so personal is how it reflects the life story and the soul of the people who live there."

OPPOSITE "We created the vaulted ceiling to make the bedroom look like a barn," says Louise. She and Daniel also installed the pine floor and the dog-eared fence boards on the walls.

RIGHT Louise embellished the antique claw-foot bathtub with a touch of her stencil work. To reflect natural light around the small room, a framed mirror hangs on the wall above the tub. Simple burlap curtains and painted flooring contribute to the vintage appeal.

BELOW A framed piece of cross-stitch by Daniel's mom adds not only an artistic touch but a personal one, too.

BELOW RIGHT Framed by trees and with a profusion of blooms on the patio, the cottage celebrates California outdoor living and the Schriddes' love of nature.

OPPOSITE Cathy has a knack for mixing pieces from various eras and provenances. Case in point, the dining room's vintage Hoosier cabinet displays an assortment of rustic stoneware and fine china. The trick is to limit accessories to give individual pieces a chance to shine.

RIGHT Keeping tableware within a cohesive palette is visually pleasing. Here, a pretty grouping of items with varied textures but similar tonality brings to mind a still-life artwork.

Southern Grace

Cathy and Jeff Collins readily admit to their infatuation with old, even dilapidated, houses. "We love historic homes and like to leave them better than when we found them," Cathy says. In 2003, they went on vacation to Eureka Springs, Arkansas. It is no surprise to learn that, while they were there, they discovered a hidden gem from 1900. Its name was Rose Cottage and they were immediately smitten by its Gothic Revival style. "It was such a stunning cottage nestled in a spectacular woodsy setting, yet only a short walk to downtown," Jeff says.

To emphasize the unique windows of the alcove, Cathy and Jeff painted the trim white while keeping the beadboard and flooring in their original colors. Their patinaed finish makes a perfect backdrop for a farmhouse table, French country chairs and rustic antiques. The window seat's elegant floral and casual burlap pillows convey a relaxed approach to style.

"That sense of authenticity is what gives a home its soul"

Courtnay Daniels

FOR YEARS, THE COUPLE TRIED to buy the home without success. "My heart kept coming back to this one-of-a-kind property. It was just magical to me, with its Gothic characteristics, inviting front porch and beautiful view," Cathy reminisces. But it wasn't until 2011, when the owner finally relented, that they were able to acquire the cottage complete with all the furnishings.

The 1,500-square-foot/140-square-meter home had been renovated in the 1980s by a couple from Texas, who eventually lost interest in it and ended up renting it to various tenants over the years. By the time Cathy and Jeff could call the cottage theirs, it had fallen into neglect. "It was stuffed full of furnishings, including some beautiful antiques, but overall, it looked too stuffy and Victorian," says Cathy. She proceeded to carefully edit each room, figuring out what to keep and what to discard. Her vision was for an airy, uncluttered feel that would bring the cottage into the 21st century.

"Our goal was to keep the historic bones, but update the cottage enough so our family and friends could be comfortable and enjoy it," she says. To that end, although she and Jeff retained the existing footprint, they added a full bathroom upstairs. "Even though it is an old home, there is an openness between the rooms that creates a natural flow from one space to the next. I love every single room in the house."

LEFT The kitchen remains true to the era of the building with its authentic walls and flooring. The farmhouse sink and scalloped shelf are original, too, but Cathy has repositioned them as the focal point. Spare furnishings, including black chairs and a white vintage wicker table, emphasize the architecture and views.

ABOVE In a cozy corner, Cathy dressed a new chair in a neutral slipcover to allow for colorful pillows. The clock and side table lend a European touch to the room.

OPPOSITE Clearing out a onetime sleeping area in the attic made way for a small writing table and chair with vintage vibes—a delightful spot to enjoy nature through the dramatic Gothic-style arched window.

For the renovation, the couple enlisted the help of local stores and craftsmen. "We like to work with small entrepreneurs," Jeff explains. "Our biggest challenge was to stay within a reasonable budget and update the infrastructure while keeping the historic integrity of the home." Cathy and Jeff were also careful to keep the beautiful blue floors and wainscoting. However, they opted to paint the walls and trim white instead of the pink and turquoise of the original design. "The white made the floor and wainscoting pop," Cathy explains.

When it comes to decorating, Cathy favors a mix of vintage, eclectic, elegant and traditional furnishings, with a touch of French country style. "I don't have a degree in interior design, but I have always loved looking at magazines and now Pinterest and Instagram," she says. "I'm pretty much self-taught. I have long loved vintage and antique items because they always have a story to tell, and I add to that story with those I find and when and where they come from. This cottage provides the perfect place to listen."

Because they wanted the period architecture to be the star of the design, the pair kept furnishings and accessories to a minimum. Finer objects are juxtaposed with primitive ones to create a personal and intentional style—and a bit of intrigue. "I chose fabrics that echoed the muted colors seen in the floors and wainscoting," says Cathy. She wanted to bring the outdoors in, so she has accentuated the natural setting with an abundance of floral patterns, including on the bed linens. To preserve the sunlit spaces and lovely views, the windows are kept mostly bare, except for a few wisps of lace.

The couple's infatuation with historic buildings has so far brought eight homes back to life. Still more are awaiting their tender, thoughtful touch. "All of our homes have been decorated from our hearts and minds," says Cathy. "We have always been attracted to houses with unique qualities and we love to restore those that have lost their soul and create a new identity that gives it back to them. I love preserving pieces of the past." She concludes: "They all tell a story." Rose Cottage is a perfect example.

OPPOSITE A wide Gothic window doubles as a grand architectural headboard for the master bedroom's Jenny Lind-style king-size bed. The color scheme in this space takes its cues from nature for a calming continuity defined by weathered finishes and floral linens.

ABOVE Facing the bed, the ornate 19th-century metal fireplace and the surrounding tiles are original to the house.

LEFT The picturesque cottage sits up on the hills overlooking downtown Eureka Springs. The period architecture and woodsy surroundings bring to mind the little homes of fairytale books.

Old Soul

As an interiors stylist, I have spent most of my career getting people's homes photo-ready for magazines and books. I have loved every visit, enjoyed working with homeowners all over the country and witnessed their happiness when they see their spaces featured in print. Their reaction is the ultimate reward. However, as much as I delight in all facets of my work, there is truly nothing I enjoy more than finally returning to my own place. Every time I come home from a trip, I fall in love with my little cottage in Sarasota, Florida all over again.

"Perhaps there is a soul hidden in
everything and it can always speak,
without even making a sound,
to another soul."

Frances Hodgson Burnett

HAVE LIVED IN SEVERAL COUNTRIES and often rented, but even then, I had to make my house a home. I have had a love affair with vintage houses, especially smaller ones, and I have always been a homebody at heart. For me, home is more than a place. It's a way of life, a mindset that's all about the story behind cherished and meaningful items. It's a comforting style that is not about spending money.

Though nestled under old oaks and surrounded by a meadow-like garden on a dead-end lane, this little home was hardly the cottage of my dreams when I first laid eyes on it. The humble façade concealed a quirky floor plan and a garish interior color scheme. Still, I was taken by the possibilities and couldn't wait to get started.

Paint has always been my best friend. It's inexpensive and such an easy way to update or transform just about anything. So, it makes sense that the process of making the cottage mine would begin with a fresh coat of paint. Maybe it's because I moved in on a luminous spring day, but instead of choosing a purely white background as I would normally do, I felt the need to include a bit of color, not just on the walls but also through the furnishings.

After painting one of the living room's walls a blush pink (Antoinette by Annie Sloan), I decided to apply the same soft hue to an old bookcase and style it with items in the same color family. In the dining area, juxtaposing white and pale blue beadboard gives the room a fresh energy. White walls united with delicate colors and whimsical patterns keep things light and inviting.

Mementos picked up on my travels and gifts from family and friends hold a special place in my heart. Maybe it's due to my French heritage and being brought up with a love for pieces valued for their history or sentimental quality. From an early age, I learned to favor the right look over the perfect pedigree. It is an authentic way of creating a home that defies the coming and going of trends and it struck a chord with me, even as a little girl. That principle remains true to this day.

My home is the keeper of my memories. I can get inspired by just about anything as long as it speaks to me. For instance, I was on a shoot in Arizona when I came across some old-fashioned eiderdowns. I brought them home as a perfectly nostalgic complement for needlepoint pillows hand-stitched by my sister.

PAGES 62 & 63 White walls and a luminous sky-blue trim highlight lush tropical blooms. Though acquired on various trips over the years, an old pail, a rusty heart and a candelabra seem made for each other.

OPPOSITE Found in a junk shop, the chandelier (a gift from my sister) adds a bit of glamour and sparkle to the eclectic mix of furnishings sourced from flea markets.

Another time, while in Texas, I found a rusty metal candelabra that had once belonged to an old church. Then there is a pair of heart-shaped candlesticks that my sister gifted me when I was visiting her in France. The list of prized items is as long as it is consequential.

There is something lovely about being surrounded by so many familiar and eloquent items in my home. They make me feel safe and give me a sense of belonging that impersonal, mass-produced objects could never achieve.

OPPOSITE & ABOVE The glass doors of the kitchen cabinets are tacked with lacy panels to hide clutter. A metallic blue chair is an eye-catching focal point. The farmhouse table was a find from Posh, a favorite shop in Venice, Florida owned by Susie and Mark Holt (see their home on pages 86–95). A collection of pale pink and blue colanders reinforces the airy palette. In the window, dish towels are clipped onto a curtain rod.

"The beautiful things in this house are meant to be touched— and meant to touch you."

LEFT An eiderdown from Sweet Salvage (a friend's shop in Arizona) and needlepoint pillows made by my sister have precious sentimental value. A farmhouse table finds a new purpose in the living room. A faux zebra-hide rug is a playful touch and keeps the room from being too sweet.

PAGE 70 Items with personal significance, such as the Cindy Redman portrait to the right of the mantel, always get pride of place. The faux fireplace was made from salvaged materials.

PAGE 71 A friend built me a rustic bookcase from leftover lumber. I added a scalloped trim, then finished the piece with Annie Sloan's petal-pink Antoinette paint. Books and objects in the same color family add a finishing touch.

Not everything has to be old, of course, as long as it holds a personal sentiment. Homemade pieces and artisanal items are a big part of my home. I got my very first heart, a gift from my mother, when I was in my teens. Over the years, I have kept on collecting them from all over the world. They are such a lovely symbol.

A home should be a poetic mix of contrasting elements that work together in harmony. It's not about displaying things just to be looked at. I once read a little sign that said, "the beautiful things in this house are meant to be touched—and meant to touch you." It perfectly sums up the way I feel about my little cottage.

ABOVE LEFT Painted beadboards, barely-there curtains and a salvaged cabinet embellished with a gathered panel give the bathroom a nostalgic grace, while a simple basin and mirror confer a hint of Zen. Baskets add texture to the otherwise monochromatic decor.

ABOVE RIGHT & OPPOSITE A painting by Rebecca Ersfeld of a sheep and her lamb speaks of my love for all animals. A mirror from my family home in Paris, a watercolor by a friend, a handmade heart, kitty Minou and a vintage eiderdown are all priceless treasures.

On the Soft Side

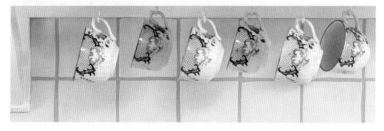

Cultivated Charm

Though they hail from different countries, Carlos Pagel and his partner
Carl Morton are united by their artistic skills and their shared passion for antiques.
Carlos is a native of Brazil whose exquisite floral installations have graced numerous
prestigious events in New York City. Carl is from Michigan—his involvement with
haute couture lead him to become the creative director for Hanae Mori, the famous
Japanese fashion designer, and later cofounder of Matsuda USA. In 1997, Carlos and
Carl added yet another phase to their creative endeavors when the industrious
duo combined and applied their talents to a new venture: interior design.

The kitchen brings then and now together. Modern cabinets feel right at home with a farmhouse sink, an antique butcher's block reborn as an island and a small bench reupholstered in a woven fabric. Hints of color warm the mainly neutral space. The vintage pendant is from Fed-On Lights in nearby Saugerties, New York.

"Innovation is often the ability to reach into the past and bring back what is good, what is beautiful, what is useful, what is lasting."

Sister Parish

OPPOSITE For a touch of contrast in the eating area, antique chairs from a New York home decorated by Sister Parish have been dressed in striped silk fabric. The pale blue shades of the chandelier, a lace tablecloth and a portrait by Norwegian artist Jorunn Mulen keep the overall look mellow.

LEFT A salvaged door is displayed in lieu of artwork. Carlos painted it with a gold heart, allowing most of the original patina to remain visible.

THE ENTERPRISING PAIR were not new to homeownership. "Our first home together was an apartment in an Art Deco building in New York's Chelsea neighborhood," Carlos recalls. "Then we headed upstate and undertook the renovation of a circa 1669 historic stone house with a large barn in Rosendale." That house became the blueprint for their decorating and collecting style, while the barn, which they filled with their newfound treasures, turned out to be the precursor to their antiques business.

When the time came to make their next move, the couple had their hearts set on a pastoral country setting. What they found was a beautiful lot with mature trees, a creek and meadow-like grounds in Woodstock, NY. "When we first saw the land, we fell in love with all the trees and the water," Carlos says. "We were lucky to find a property like this in such close proximity to town."

The couple designed a new 2,000-square-foot/186-square-meter home (including a wraparound porch) and had it built to their specifications. "It was an easy decision," Carlos recalls. "We wanted a classic American cottage that would evoke the country lifestyle through the use of vintage furniture, floral textiles, wallpapers (both current and vintage), a dash of shabby chic and mementos of our lives, family and friends all around."

Now complete, the home has a fresh and thoughtful design with vaulted ceilings, a cozy stone fireplace, wide-plank oak flooring and a profusion of French doors. "Coming from a dark house, we definitely wanted as much light as possible," says Carl.

LEFT Despite its 18-foot/5.5-meter-high vaulted ceiling, the living room feels intimate thanks to a sofa and love seat set between the fireplace with a mantel made from an old beam and a wall of bookcases. A salvaged trunk, vintage nesting tables and artworks by Jorunn Mulen and Japanese painter Minol Araki establish a sense of timelessness.

"Coming from a dark house, we definitely wanted as much light as possible."

Defined by an aesthetically pleasing and calm interior with a flowingly lyrical yet subtle manner, Carl and Carlos's home is an ode to their shared love of vintage. A core palette of creams, whites and grays sets the peaceful backdrop for furnishings and establishes the couple's fondness for gentle shades of lilac, blush, cloud blue and buttery yellow. Nature provided a helping hand along the way. "We painted most of the interior in variations of a lichen color by Benjamin Moore," Carlos explains. "We were so inspired by the surrounding trees that we actually took a piece of lichen-covered bark to the paint store to match it."

Textures and natural materials also contribute to the refined country style of the cottage. The couple have edited their spaces so that everything has room to breathe, allowing them to showcase the characteristics of each piece. From the soft tones of a painting to the fabric of a throw pillow, from the fragrance of a scented candle to a plethora of meaningful mementos, all facets of the decor feel more collected than coordinated.

"I've been inspired by many people and styles, especially Rachel Ashwell and Sister Parish," Carlos says. "We kept some furniture and artwork from our previous home, but this house took on a life of its own.

We aimed for a soft, romantic, cozy look with a depth of nostalgia achieved by the use of antiques and art." This union carries on the past while adding to the couple's ongoing story in the present. "For two homebodies who appreciate these qualities in a home, it's essential to be visually stimulated and comfortable at the same time," Carl adds.

Even the grounds received careful attention. Forsythia and fragrant creeping thyme line the driveway. A path of bluestone bedrock, carefully unearthed to show its striations, leads to a grand wraparound porch designed for alfresco meals. On both sides of the front steps, rose bushes and pear and crab apple trees keep company with other plantings.

Though their home is not old, Carlos and Carl have incorporated distinctive elements to add a sense of timeless comfort. Their warm, inviting approach to decoration is in perfect harmony with their philosophy of intentional living. Together they have created a cohesive loveliness with a charmingly faded flair.

OPPOSITE Carl and Carlos have a fondness for items with their original finish, like this antique dresser/chest of drawers in a faded buttercup hue. The top offers just the right surface to display an endearing vignette composed of a delicate Murano mirror, floral artwork and a marble-footed lamp.

ABOVE RIGHT While searching for shades for an antique Limoges lamp, Carlos found this blue-trimmed pair on Etsy.

RIGHT The bathroom's glamorous marble-topped vanity from RH is paired with an ornate mirror and fanciful Brockhampton Star wallpaper by Farrow & Ball.

The dining room captures the easy spirit of beachside living. Windows provide an unobstructed panorama of the beach and playful marine life. With a handmade table paired with a crystal chandelier and the union of garden chairs with a rustic bench, the mix of decor elements bears Susie's coastal-chic fingerprints.

RIGHT Local shells, such as these satiny ones, make beautiful decor. "It's amazing what we find on the beach," says Susie.

Seaside Oasis

"Living in Florida, it's always been our dream to have a small beach cottage," says Sarasota native Susie Holt. "We longed for something authentic and charming and with a great view." When Susie and her husband Mark began their search for a quaint home, they found exactly what they were looking for: a little old house overlooking the white-sand beach of a barrier island. The spell was cast instantly.

The sign reads: *Beach is where the home is*

SUSIE AND MARK FOUNDED their vintage home furnishings store Posh over 25 years ago in nearby Venice. They immediately spotted the many period features that make this 1920s cottage unique. "With its vintage windows, original hardwood floors and panoramic view, this little shack is one of the oldest cottages here on Casey Key—it is pure Old Florida," Susie explains. To which Mark is quick to add: "Historic cottages are priceless. People don't fix these up anymore. They demolish them and build mansions because the land is so valuable."

The couple wondered if the 1,000-square-foot/ 93-square-meter home would accommodate their furniture, which held much sentimental value. But it proved to be much bigger than it seems. For Susie and Mark, besides the location, the cottage's appeal is its simplicity. "It only has one bedroom, one bathroom and a tiny kitchen, but the spacious living/dining room makes up for it," says Susie. "It has a 20-foot/6-meter expanse of windows facing the Gulf of Mexico."

LEFT "I love white!" exclaims Susie, whose slipcovered sofas epitomize easy care. Chipped paint on cabinets and an antique shutter creates a beachy, weather-worn appeal. The bare wooden tabletop evokes driftwood, especially when paired with starfish and blue goblets that are reminiscent of seaglass.

LEFT & OPPOSITE An antique screen door between the living room and kitchen keeps the homey, vintage vibe flowing. Former bookcases now play the role of a pantry, offering much-needed storage. The linoleum floor is original to the house.

ABOVE To take advantage of the inspiring views, whether of the surrounding flora or the coastline, Susie keeps window treatments to a minimum. Here, a vintage tablecloth makes a dainty statement.

The couple worked together to transform the little cottage into their dream home. Susie is known for her layered, serene beach-chic aesthetic, which became the foundation for the home makeover. "We wanted a pure palette, so we started by painting all the walls white. I knew I would bring in inspiration from the water, so all our accents would be in aqua. I wanted everything to be beach-easy, with no fuss," she says.

The rooms reflect their affinity for treasured family heirlooms and pieces with history, such as intricately framed mirrors that Susie will never part with. A dresser/chest of drawers is adorned with her trademark artisanal, one-of-a-kind pieces and architectural finds that they collected on their trips around the country— an early 1900s mirror from Belgium, crystal chandeliers from France, a screen door from Savannah, Georgia, embellished with a carved wooden seahorse—all united with coastal references that echo the waterside location.

OPPOSITE The curvaceous king-size iron bed frame is one of Susie's favorite finds. She layers textures in pillow shams, Bella Notte bed linen and diaphanous curtains to establish a sanctuary-like feel. The weathered shutter and original wood floor add depth to the pristine yet inviting space.

ABOVE & RIGHT The small bathroom accommodates a narrow foyer where fresh towels are kept handy, and a recess for a vintage mirror and a vanity. A simple metal garden chair and a sparkling crystal chandelier illustrate Susie's characterful interpretation of high-low style.

In every space, light, ever-changing water views and Susie's skills as an interior designer come to play. Oversized and overstuffed with down, sofas and chairs in breezy white muslin slipcovers offer style and substance. Elegant chandeliers contrast with rustic elements like an old coffee table with chippy white paintwork, while vintage bottles and aqua glass accents evoke a sense of sea and sand. "The bedroom is exactly how a bedroom should be: tranquil and peaceful," Susie says. "I chose the white palette because it evokes serenity." The entire space is dedicated to calm and beauty. Airy curtains, soft blankets and elegant furniture soothe the senses, just like the sounds of ocean waves outside the window.

The kitchen is the perfect union of style and function. "Even though it is small, it is part of what the cottage is: cozy and simple in an artful way," Susie says. "It fits our life perfectly. Nothing makes me happier than looking out to the water as I prepare our meals."

Mark is a skilled carpenter and it is his job to repair and restore the pieces that they find and those passed on from friends and family. "But not to a perfect state," he notes. "Chips, cracks and dings are marks of beauty." He also excels at building new furniture from recycled elements. His projects include the 8-foot/2.5-meter dining table, which he constructed with legs that were once porch posts, and the built-in kitchen cabinets made from salvaged wood. "Mixing in vintage and artisanal finds makes the rooms feel cozier and more personal," he adds.

From working side by side in their store to thoughtfully creating their home, Mark and Susie have surrounded themselves with things that speak to them and of them, making their little cottage a joyful and meaningful oasis.

RIGHT With a beach as their front yard, Mark and Susie spend time there daily. Sturdy Adirondack chairs offer a cozy spot to watch saturated sunsets and the tides rolling in. Collecting shells provides instant stress relief, and relaxing after a day's work is a key element of the laid-back island lifestyle. In Susie's words, "This is good for the soul."

Natural fabrics and wood tones bring authenticity and an organic feel to Laurie's home. The white-on-white scheme is luminescent in the sunlight, offering a cool contrast to the desert landscape. The most precious collections in this house are personal, not pricey. Stones gathered on family hikes and painted by Laurie and her children mark time spent together.

Artful Adobe

With its rich history, picturesque Pueblo-style architecture, spectacular scenery and spiritual community, Santa Fe, New Mexico is known as one of America's most fascinating cities. And its prominence as a mecca for artists didn't go unnoticed by jewelry designer Laurie Lenfestey, who established residence in one of the city's most significant historic neighborhoods 25 years ago.

THERE IS A PROVERB THAT SAYS, "He who has not tasted bitter cannot taste sweet." This is something Laurie understands. She has a keen sense of the passage of time and looks at life as a collage filled with bits and pieces and tinted with a bittersweet aura. "Mostly sweet with a hint of sadness," she explains. That sentiment was rendered especially acute from watching her children William and Olivia growing up. What began with making sweet little cards to put in their lunch boxes transformed into an unexpected business, documenting and saving moments and events in their lives.

"I first made my son a book filled with collages based around who he was," Laurie recalls. "He loved it and we shared it with other moms. They wanted me to make them for their children, too, and I saw a need I could fill." The demand grew over time and before long Laurie had created an extensive line of custom journals, wedding albums, baby books and more. "Back then, the children would often help with the production and assembly, such as gluing cabochons and ribbons to the books' collages," Laurie reminisces. "It was just the sweetest time."

Shiny and elegant items temper rougher and earthier ones throughout the home. "It's about the beauty of contrasts," Laurie explains. "A case in point, my friend Dawn Sweitzer of Notre Monde crafted the dining-room table with its weathered wood base and also the beveled mirror." The crystal chandelier adds a glamorous vibe.

Laurie hails from Rhode Island where Providence, the state's capital, happens to be known as the costume jewelry capital of the world. While on a visit back to her home state, Laurie was looking for vintage baubles to embellish her creations. As luck would have it, she came across a milky-white rosary and fell in love with the beads. "I bought 150 pounds of these beauties and that's how my jewelry line got its start," she recalls. Since its inception in 2005, Bittersweet Designs on Canyon Road has evolved into one of Santa Fe's most beloved shops. The exquisite artisanal handmade jewelry collections have all been inspired by Laurie's personal stories of growth and discovery. Just like the jewelry she creates, Laurie's home is an assemblage of sentimental mementos and curated pieces that reflect her deep family ties and life's journey.

TOP LEFT & ABOVE LEFT Laurie sets small collectibles under glass cloches on the dining-room table and surrounds them with candles and flowers in clear jars and vases to create impactful one-of-a-kind centerpieces.

ABOVE Creating richly textured assemblages from rustic and refined elements is a defining characteristic of Laurie's signature style. In this display, she relies on symmetry to confer a subtle harmony.

In the living room, a salvaged mirror and a cutout banister used as a screen add graphic beauty to the original fireplace. Carved spindles transformed into candlesticks provide sculptural shapes. For a dramatic display, Laurie has lined up slender apothecary jars to show off more of the family's natural collections.

"An interior is the natural projection of the soul."

Coco Chanel

PAGE 102 Multiple French doors usher in the light and the view while giving the family easy access to quiet courtyards beyond. The monochromatic interiors keep the focus on the natural world outside.

PAGE 103 Daughter Olivia's bedroom gets a graceful, feminine lift from a sheer canopy of mosquito netting. Hints of color bring soft yet subtle contrast to the little girl's dreamy space.

"Everything I do is a collage," says the artist. "I love putting things together: jewelry, spaces and even people. It's all about how things complement one another."

She cites her upbringing as a major influence on her style. "My mom inspired my neutral aesthetic," she says. "Her home was always peaceful, and she had a knack for making everything beautiful and everyone welcome." Though her parents have passed away, they remain a feature of Laurie's life. She set up an altar in a nook off her dining room with their photographs, letters and other meaningful mementos. "It's just a little place where I can go and be with them," she explains.

Throughout the home, creamy plastered walls are the perfect backdrop for weathered furniture, gleaming accessories and natural elements. These subtle layers of texture imbue the interior with unusual partnerships and plenty of intrigue. "A monochromatic palette becomes more interesting when united with timeworn pieces, woven fabrics and grainy woods," Laurie notes.

Displaying sentimental objects—such as the stones gathered on walks with her children and five antique cherubs that represent Laurie and her siblings—underlines her evocative decorating. "I don't collect just things, I collect memories and meanings. I'm not much of a shopper, so most of my collections come from travels, experiences and nature." Her aesthetic flows from one room to the next with a soothing simplicity that creates a sense of serenity and visual continuity.

Laurie is fascinated by architectural buildings and reclaimed fragments. In her home, classic Santa Fe elements speak of her affection for traditional vernacular architecture. Rough-hewn beams known as vigas and Pueblo fireplaces called kivas bring their character into the space along with her various salvaged pieces and collections. The interior is at once nuanced and sophisticated. Simple, clean-lined furniture dressed in white cotton and linen coexists with mirrors, sparkling crystal chandeliers and sconces, vintage columns, wooden santos figurines and other storied heirlooms and artifacts.

When she settled in New Mexico, Laurie brought with her the knowledge she gained from working in Boston for the National Trust for Historic Preservation. "When I moved here, I wanted to include a bit of my roots within the architecture of my Santa Fe home," explains the New England native. Laurie genuinely believes that when you go with what you love, it works beautifully because it comes from an authentic place. "For me, creating a home that looks good and feels good is all about the blending of things that have meaning to us," she says. "When considerate layers of memories celebrating life's milestones are present, the soul of a home becomes evident. Here we can listen to life's whispers."

ABOVE RIGHT Gleaming mirrors, sparkling pendants and layers of cloud-soft bedding bring a quiet elegance to the master bedroom. True to Laurie's aesthetic, color and pattern take a second seat to textural interest.

RIGHT In a little nook, a kiva fireplace and cushy pillows invite quiet moments while enhancing the bedroom's charm and comfort.

OPPOSITE Though the bathroom follows Laurie's style, it takes on a glamorous vibe with marble tiles and a chandelier, proving that luxury and practicality can be close allies.

3

Artistic Inclinations

LEFT A talented artist in his own right, Carol's husband Mike used recycled wood to make this sign sporting the name of her business, as well as the filing cabinet on which it is propped.

OPPOSITE Beadboard that was discovered in the walls during the garage renovation was carefully salvaged and used to make the doors of the kitchen cabinets. A pair of internal windows was transformed into chalkboards to mask the view into the laundry room. Shelves are lined with majolica ceramics, one of Carol's collecting passions.

Tattered Treasure

It's so perfectly fitting how the name and style of textile artist Carol Riley reflect the expression "the life of Riley." Everything about her home in Bristol, Rhode Island exudes easygoing, carefree charm. A native of Dublin, Carol moved here in the 1980s with her English-born husband Mike, a world squash referee and coach. "It's the longest we've lived anywhere," says Carol.

> "Stick to things you really
> love. An honest room is
> always up to date."
>
> Billy Baldwin

OPPOSITE & RIGHT A candelabra that lived outdoors for a while appeals to Carol's love of things with character and history. A lampshade trimmed with whimsical pompoms makes a delightfully unique light fixture.

PAGES 112-113 Carol sees the potential in everything. When she came across an ugly Victorian sofa covered in pink satin, she removed the fabric and remade the seat cushions with fabric remnants. Ikea room dividers serve as window shutters. Mike drilled the holes to let light peek through.

N BETWEEN RAISING FOUR CHILDREN, the couple have done a lot of work on the 2,000-square-foot/186-square-meter cottage over the years. They have brought in vintage details and well-worn character, and incorporated many personal mementos.

Though the house is more than 80 years old, Carol considers it young compared to buildings back in the old country. She recalls being instantly drawn to the cottage for its charming shape, architectural features and yard full of cherry blossom trees. "With its front door centered between two windows and a porch draped with roses, the exterior looked like a kid's drawing," Carol says. "It reminded us of the cottages of Devon and Cornwall in England." However, the interior was in dire need of improvements, both structural and cosmetic. "It

was quite simply ugly, with loads of fake panels and other unsightly and deteriorating materials," says Carol.

As the couple set out to improve and beautify the quaint home, they made a great team. "Mike is amazing—he goes along with my ideas and makes them happen. He is self-taught and brilliant." Carol herself is blessed with an enviable ability to see possibilities where others might see nothing at all. A drab old sofa, a bland kitchen cabinet, a simple lampshade frame—all have ugly-duckling potential in her eyes. "It's wonderful to transform pieces," she observes. "But the downside of that is that it's hard for me to throw anything away!"

Carol's resourcefulness came to the fore during the renovations when she and Mike discovered real beadboard panels hidden behind the garage walls.

The bedroom's color scheme is inspired by the masses of
hydrangeas that grow right outside. The extra-tall bed not
only has a dramatic presence but it also offers plenty of
storage beneath for stashing Carol's many textiles.
Contemporary linens from Designers Guild make a
charming canvas for a collection of handmade pillows
fashioned from old blankets and tablecloths. The side table
is a kitchen cabinet covered with salvaged beadboard.

"I have loved fabrics, especially vintage ones, since I was little."

"We saved every bit in all its glorious scrappy blue and gray colors," she explains. This salvaged material has found a new life as kitchen cabinetry and as cladding for the bathroom walls.

She also has no qualms about refurbishing a preloved item with vintage materials that respect its origin. Another time, she instructed Mike to cut the arms off an old sofa that she had picked up at the Salvation Army store for $40. "It turned out fabulous once I ripped off the fabric, painted the wooden frame and made new cushions and pillows," she says. "I'm a little bit fearless that way. When the moment hits me that I want to make something, I'm going to go ahead and do it."

One of her more unusual projects was wallpapering a bedroom floor, with unexpected results. "The wallpaper got stained, so I painted over it, and now it has rubbed off in parts and it almost looks like old concrete. Who could have predicted that?"

To complete the casual, comfortable and inviting interior, Carol and Mike chose to include numerous rescued finds, salvaged items and personal heirlooms. For instance, the dining room's trestle table once belonged to Carol's dad. Ever resourceful, she managed to bring it over from England in pieces in the family suitcases.

The cottage is an inspirational setting for Carol to work on her design business, Tatters. "I have loved fabrics, especially vintage ones, since I was little," she explains. "I do a bit of everything: clothing, furnishings, bags and jewelry. I'm constantly changing things around. It's not that I get bored, it's just that my mind is always working."

ABOVE LEFT & RIGHT Carol embellished the frame of a lampshade with spangles, buttons and beads, and used salvaged crewelwork from her stash of treasured fabrics to create beautiful throw pillows.

OPPOSITE Though it resembles a charming old gate, the backdrop to the porch sofa is actually a 1970s headboard revived with paint. The wreath on the wall above was built on a picture frame, with layers of buttons and beads strung together. The exotic hanging lantern was a bargain from an auction.

It's the same creative drive that compelled Carol to transform an old church in nearby Warren into her very own tearoom and boutique named The Church Palace. With the help of the entire Riley family, she has achieved remarkable results.

Whether it's clothing or rooms, Carol is an expert at bringing in a mix of salvaged, handmade and reimagined elements. Following her love of things that transcend time and place, the Irish maverick and her enterprising husband have turned a once-forgotten cottage and an abandoned church into considered and artful spaces. Both are filled with items that keep pieces of the past alive and celebrate their original stories with both functionality and soul.

Organic Vibes

Donna Morgan's love of baubles and relics of all kinds began in early childhood and ended up being the foundation of her artistic pursuits. "I've always been a collector, weaving fragments of the past into unique, sustainable treasures," she says. Discarded jewelry finds a new life under her fingertips, while salvaged fabrics blossom into one-of-a-kind bags. Each piece whispers a story born from her imagination and repurposed with love.

THE WORLD IS DONNA'S CANVAS, and every encounter a brushstroke. But her creativity goes far beyond the pieces she dreams up, and her California home is no exception. "My friend Francisco Delgado, who is also an artist, had built a cabana-like hideaway in his backyard in Tarzana. It was a little sanctuary where he could go and meditate," she recalls. At the time it was a rudimentary structure with only three walls. However, when the opportunity arose for her to live there, she immediately saw the possibilities and her visionary gift went into overdrive. "My first priority was to expand the tiny footprint while respecting the original design, which had been constructed using only architectural salvage and found materials." The plan was to add a bedroom alcove with a dressing area and a bathroom. However, there was an obstacle to overcome: a tree growing right where the new rooms were slated to go. "Instead of cutting it, we just build around it!"

"A room should feel
collected, not decorated."

Albert Hadley

PAGES 118 & 119 Salvaged windows, shutters and
doors are just a few of the eco-friendly materials
used to build the tree house-like sanctuary.

LEFT Donna collects vintage and antique crosses,
which she displays individually or, as here, in pairs.

BELOW LEFT & RIGHT Fashioned into a stand,
bleached driftwood holds bracelets and necklaces
handmade by Donna. A vintage door hung from the
rafters becomes a distinctive light fixture with
candles similar in shape and color.

OPPOSITE Donna creates evocative vignettes with
personal mementos, objects and thoughtful notes
that share textures, tones, shapes and, most of all, a
meaningful theme that fits her soulful aesthetic.

KEEP YOUR FEARS TO YOURSELF,
BUT SHARE YOUR INSPIRATION
WITH OTHERS. Robert Louis Stevenson

"They're not just objects; they're fragments of my journey and tangible reminders of my life."

And so, it began. Piece by recycled piece, the former cabana morphed into the dream retreat Donna had envisioned. The front steps were made with old railroad ties/railway sleepers. Other reclaimed architectural elements include the weathered wooden shingles and old windows and doors. Today, the building is at one with its surroundings, in accordance with Donna's artistic ethos. She loves to blend elements of nature with unexpected and diverse textures, creating a uniquely personal aesthetic.

"Nature engages your senses in a particular way," she notes. "The colors of wildflowers, the sound of birdsong and the earthy scent of lavender and sage all combine to create a stimulating and immersive experience that sparks joy and appreciation." Throughout the interior, succulents are given pride of place because they hold a special significance for Donna. "They are much more than decoration—they are miniature ecosystems, thriving testaments to nature's quiet strength and adaptability," she explains. "Looking at them, I'm reminded that beauty can bloom even in the toughest conditions, and that a touch of organic life can awaken awareness in anyone who enters the room."

LEFT Antique wrought-iron corbels, along with a pair of draped vintage sheets, frame the entrance to the bedroom. Donna added the lace tablecloth under the bed for textural contrast. The curvaceous planter was purchased in Mexico and made into a nightstand/bedside table with the addition of a tiled top.

ABOVE A table made from miscellaneous parts, including an old barrel, rests in the crook of the indigenous tree around which the bedroom area was built.

OPPOSITE By adding a basin, a slab of marble and new plumbing, a found antique Chinese chest has been reimagined into a handsome vanity in the bathroom area. The suspended wooden shelf is another find that now holds seashells, flowers and rosary beads.

Though the interior boasts an array of white items, color is very much part of the scheme. "I don't know why, but I always end up adding turquoise to everything," Donna muses. Various shades of wood—from the barn doors in the living room to the bathroom vanity, the workspace table and the repurposed French armoire—come into focus as well. "For me, homes aren't just shelters; they're living entities with their own energy and spirit," she says. "The belief that these havens choose their residents, rather than the other way around, resonates deeply with me."

Looking around her home, it's evident that Donna is much more than a jewelry maker: she is a treasure hunter, a storyteller and a second-chance advocate. She weaves magic out of the ordinary, breathing new life into discarded items and giving each piece a voice to tell their stories and share their history and meaning through her designs.

When asked if she has a favorite sentimental object, she is quick to answer. "Pinpointing a single item is impossible because each one speaks to a part of my soul. Each piece has a story, not of its material form but of a fleeting emotion, a cherished memory or a unique experience. They're not just objects; they're fragments of my journey and tangible reminders of my life."

As the final touches were placed, for Donna it was a part of herself that was completed, as well as her home and her artwork. "In that moment, I saw not just the creation but a reflection of me and all that I hold dear. It was a beautiful revelation, like gazing into a mirror that unveiled my very soul." It's safe to say that the anthem of Donna's life is thriving in her evocative home.

LEFT, TOP & ABOVE Next to an antique armoire, a large standing mirror reflects back the room, creating an illusion of spaciousness. Cupboard doors are put to use to display jewelry and accessories.

OPPOSITE A sunken bathtub doubles as a shower. Bathing sundries rest casually, yet practically, on a built-in ledge. A crown hook on the tree trunk functions as a towel holder. Potted and hanging plants add to the greenhouse effect.

LEFT A ladder is at once useful and charming as both a place to hold a quilt and hat, and to serve as wall decor. Macrame fringe adds to the boho vibe.

OPPOSITE Rather than replacing the kitchen wall cabinets with new ones, Kate simply removed the doors. Salvaged wood planks were used to clad the wall around the tiled backsplash. The freestanding work surface to the left of the sink was an old biology lab bench that Kate refreshed with dark paint and brass hardware; it now houses pots and utensils with style.

A Second Chance

Not everyone has the good fortune to get to live in their childhood home as adults. California native Kate Keesee is one of the lucky few. But again, not everyone has such a unique and loving relationship as Kate shared with her mother. "My mom, who was an unmarried woman, adopted me and raised me on her own. When I turned 18, she put me on the house title deed and had me pay toward the mortgage every month," Kate recalls. "Later in life, she gifted me her half of the home and the property became mine. I never forgot how she took care of me, encouraged me and taught me the value of working toward owning this home."

"Blessed are they who see
beautiful things in humble
places where other
people see nothing."

Camille Pissarro

LEFT The door-less cabinets now provide the open shelving Kate always wanted for a fraction of the cost of buying new.

OPPOSITE With space at a premium in the tiny kitchen, Kate constructed a second ladder to display a handmade macramé garland and to keep towels handy. She also built wooden shelves from old fence posts that she found in an alley to add storage and show off her favorite collections.

THAT UPBRINGING IS AT THE VERY CORE of Kate's creative and nurturing lifestyle. "I lost my mother last year," she explains. "Our story was about second chances. She was the one person who, since my youth, instilled empathy for others in me—she served faithfully in the senior community for over 30 years. My mother also encouraged the fact that I had a great eye for details and for selecting items. She cheered me on in all my endeavors. Even as a child she allowed me to change my room constantly."

That empathy for others motivated Kate to create Salvage Dior, a sustainable marketplace. All the proceeds go to help widowed seniors in honor of her mother. "It makes me feel connected to her in so many ways."

Everything in her Anaheim home is handmade or remade by Kate, who uses recycled materials and secondhand furniture for all her projects. Her aesthetic is a mix of eco, glamour, rustic and contemporary. "I'm definitely an out-of-the-box thinker, and I choose things that speak to me," she says. "For many years I rescued and restored roadside finds and sold them to friends."

Kate worked for 25 years as a wedding planner, a career she describes as "very demanding and high pressure." In her spare time, she channeled her skills into making the house beautiful for herself and her children on a tight budget. Then she was diagnosed with lupus, a chronic inflammatory disease, and her budget got even smaller.

Ever resilient and resourceful, Kate continued to blog about her flea-market finds and decorating projects. "My audience was the everyday woman, like me, with a dream to beautify her home on a shoestring," she says. "I spent countless hours connecting with people who wanted to do the same with little monetary means."

After suffering a small stroke in 2015, Kate decided it was time to walk away from the wedding industry. "After rehabilitation, I pivoted to my true passion: interior design." And when she joined Instagram and went from posting snapshots to pulling out power tools and showing what she was making, her account grew by leaps and bounds. She now has close to 150,000 enthusiastic followers eager to be inspired by her low-cost high-end schemes.

Kate believes the secret to her success is being fully transparent with her followers. She shares openly how to create a home on the tiniest budget and where to source materials or preowned items, and encourages others to use what they already have.

OPPOSITE Nearly everything in the neutral living room was either sourced at the Goodwill or made from salvaged wood. Wispy window treatments allow intricate pieces such as the tasseled wall hanging and vintage chandelier to star. Religious pieces are among Kate's favorite items to collect.

ABOVE The bricks of the fireplace were revived with a fresh coat of white paint and the mantel reconfigured with two hefty beams painted in the same color. To give the hearth a timeworn appearance, Kate used large reclaimed planks, which she has painted and distressed.

LEFT A found desk was revived with white paint; the Mexican equipale barrel-style chair draped in macramé was discovered in a dumpster/skip. A barn door crafted by Mom's Garage Woodworking brings a textural contrast to the simple space.

ABOVE Objects with patina pair well with frilly greenery. Kate often drills holes through wooden vessels for use as plant pots.

"At the beginning, I had only one space to use, a freshly painted family room, so it became my blank canvas," she explains. Each week she would style and create a new look using her thrift-store finds and share with her fans.

"I did this for about six months, until one day I received an email from a large retail company asking if I was really recreating the same space over and over again, or styling in multiple homes. I wrote back that I indeed was using and reinventing the same space," she recalls. "They were amazed at how each design concept was so different and offered me a paid year-long partnership." That opened the door to a flood of offers that allowed her to turn her passion for interiors into a full-time endeavor. "I'm always grateful for that first break." Kate says.

Like her mother, Kate is a lover of second chances. "Though I'm definitely more minimalist, I have an old soul and love creating an earthy, rustic style," she says. "Everything in my home has been curated over time. Whether I made it myself, found it curbside or bought it from a thrift store, it spoke to me, and I brought it here to be loved."

Western culture is represented by *King of the Hill*, a favorite print from CC + Mike, which Kate framed using reclaimed wood. A trio of graphic pillows hails from With Lavender and Grace. The baskets, lamp and bench cushion are from thrift stores.

OPPOSITE The blush-rose mural by D. Marie Interiors was the inspiration for the guest room. "Then I was in a serious hunt for everything else," says Kate. She soon spotted the brand-new tapestry area rug at a resale shop. The dream catcher made by Kate's friend Mary has sentimental value.

ABOVE "A little rustic touch never loses its magic. I love giving new life to old fence wood," Kate says, pointing to the headboard she constructed with scraps. Crisp white bedding topped with pale chenille blankets softens the look without being frilly. A rescued table keeps books handy for bedtime reading.

RIGHT & FAR RIGHT Kate creates wall art pieces using fragments of rescued wood and various hardware parts—resulting in artisanal assemblages that enliven the walls with an organic, homespun quality.

4

Nesting Instincts

LEFT Silhouette profiles, a popular way to capture portraits before photography became widespread, fill the gallery wall with family history and nostalgic charm. The horizontal mirror acts as a focal point and also adds light and movement to the dark painted wall.

OPPOSITE The 12-foot/3.7-meter-deep wraparound porch is the family's favorite feature of the cabin. Darryl constructed the swinging bed using barn wood from a local mill, while Annie made it cozy with throws and pillows. Metal plumbing pipes support the drop-cloth curtains.

Cabin Class

If one home tells the story of its owners perfectly, it has to be that of Darryl McCreary, a master craftsman, and his wife Annie, an accomplished seamstress. A few years ago, the couple decided to build a house on their family's property in Leiper's Fork, Tennessee. They had their hearts set on a classically rustic style that would stand the test of time and fit the needs of their family now and later.

OPPOSITE Annie keeps the kitchen uncluttered and easy to navigate. The ample sink was another Darryl find—he pulled it from an old farmhouse basement and then mounted it to sturdy vintage stair balusters. Annie made a curtain from French grain sacks to cover the base.

"Your home should tell the story of who you are and be a collection of what you love."

Nate Berkus

THE COUPLE AGREED THAT A CABIN was the right choice, so they began searching for the perfect floor plan. When they couldn't find a suitable one, Darryl's skills took over. "We felt this would be our forever home and knew the main level had to include everything we would require as we got older," Annie explains. "But we also needed our three boys Aidan, Liam and Finn to have their own private spaces while they were still living at home. Darryl drew up the ideal plan in a few minutes, including a full basement with three bedrooms, a living room and bathroom." The boys, now adults, lived happily in this area until they were ready to move on.

With their plan in hand, the couple proceeded with the construction of their 3,100-square-foot/290-square-meter cabin using insulating concrete forms to ensure durability and longevity. "Darryl wanted the efficiency of modern convenience, but we both love a traditional style that would age gracefully and complement the woodsy setting," Annie says. To fulfill both wishes, they chose to clad the concrete exterior with rough oak board-and-batten siding and added oversize porches overlooking the surrounding woods. "We love the views and consider our porches to be extra living spaces," Annie says.

A testament to Darryl and Annie's talents, the cabin features his and her handiwork inside and out along with some clever twists—plumbing pipes and knobs repurposed as curtain rods and cabinet pulls, a birdcage made into a light fixture and a corrugated metal panel salvaged from Darryl's parents' barn becoming a focal wall, to name a few.

Meanwhile, Annie's sewing skills are put to practical use throughout the house in the form of laundry-friendly curtains and slipcovers for chairs and feather-stuffed sofas. She also excels at mingling pieces from different eras thanks to shared qualities such as metallic shine, graphic details and sculptural forms.

"Having a small budget actually makes you a bit more creative and resourceful. It forces you to use what you have," says Annie, who lives by the mantra "Make do and mend." While she strives to keep things functional, her passion for lush textiles is evident.

LEFT A wall painted deep gray frames a dining area in the open space while providing a dramatic showcase for assorted family heirlooms. A four-poster bed turned into a table by Darryl accommodates large gatherings of friends and family. Retro steel chairs echo the corrugated metal cladding on the adjacent wall.

"We both love a traditional style that would age gracefully and complement the woodsy setting."

ABOVE Annie adores exotic patterns, rustic elements and textural accents, which range from farmhouse to funky. Persian rugs, mudcloth pillows and furry throws convey a rustic-meets-refined vibe.

OPPOSITE An old birdcage wired into a light fixture, an antique mirror and a pedestal bathtub (found on Craigslist) conspire to give the new bathroom timeless character and nostalgic vintage style.

Thick rugs, colorful quilts, blankets with whimsical trims and layers of velvets and linens are scattered throughout the cabin, adding comfort and charm. And the few pieces that Annie and Darryl did not fabricate themselves are either family items or flea-market finds that have withstood plenty of wear and tear.

A big kitchen was one of two top priorities on Annie's list. "We love having parties and entertaining. Everyone ends up in the kitchen around the island and on the porches," she says. The other was the main bedroom and bathroom. "My home is my refuge, and my bedroom is the comfiest spot to recharge. Darryl doesn't even fuss over how many pillows I have on the bed anymore!"

Family history is a defining element of McCreary style. Annie's parents were antiques collectors and dealers. "They have greatly influenced my aesthetic," she says.

"I have loved anything with a history since I was a child. If ever I need anything for my house, I always opt for vintage or custom made."

Annie loves creating an inviting and meaningful home. And though she favors beautiful things, they also have to be practical. "Raising three boys and having pets in the house means that my home has to be livable and unfussy," she explains, which is why the rustic style appeals to her. Her aesthetic is pretty, but not too perfect: think tarnished silver, chipped china plates, scuffed tables and frayed linen.

"I wanted a peaceful and comfortable home filled with priceless mementos," she explains. "Every time I use my mom's dishes or my dad's cast-iron skillet, I feel their presence. They're all around me and it helps to remind me where I came from and who I am."

Annie believes that when people live in harmony with the history behind the items they own, a home emits a particular feeling. "I couldn't imagine not having my family pieces around me. It would be like living in a body with no soul."

LEFT Darryl made the bedroom's wooden headboard and Annie sewed the ruffled bed linen. The elegant antique Drexel Heritage nightstands/bedside tables were inherited from Darryl's grandmother.

Tiny Heaven

Rhode Island is a small state with a unique blend of rich history, beautiful shoreline and a vibrant artistic community. When mother and daughter Pamela and Ara Millette were looking for a coastal summer getaway, they found a tiny yet intriguing cottage in the picturesque seaside village of Wakefield. The duo knew that the little home, built in 1957 with a footprint of just 285 square feet/26.5 square meters, would need a complete overall. With that goal in mind, they sought the expertise of interior designer Bernadette Heydt.

BERNADETTE FOUNDED HER COMPANY Heydt Home with her husband Andrea Pietrangeli, a contractor and master carpenter, who played a pivotal role in overseeing the construction work on the cottage. The project became a family affair, with Bernadette's father Bill and Andrea's uncle Mauro Lisotti joining forces to lend their expertise and support. Their combined efforts underscored the project's sentimental value, marking a treasured moment of familial bond and collaboration. And soon, the transformation of the mid-century cottage into a modern, fully functional family home began.

"In Rhode Island, giving your home a name is a cherished tradition—it's a delightful way to connect to the local culture and distinct atmosphere of this area," explains Bernadette, who is based in Newport.

"May your home always
be too small to hold all
of your friends."

Irish proverb

"When we selected the name Sea La Vie, we aimed to capture the family's relaxed lifestyle while also paying tribute to their French-Canadian heritage."

Bernadette and Andrea are known for creating bespoke spaces that exude a sense of mindful living, embracing individuality and creativity. Their signature style is characterized by clean lines, a neutral color palette, rich textures and an unwavering commitment to optimizing the potential of small spaces. "We specialize in crafting interior spaces that celebrate the beauty of simplicity." Bernadette says. "Our design ethos revolves around the transformative power of minimalism, where less becomes more and functionality blends seamlessly with style."

The interior of Sea La Vie is a captivating fusion of simplicity and coastal chic. Designing a tiny home requires thoughtful solutions in order to fit all the utilities that modern living demands. "We had to be strategic with the layout and maximize the use of the available square footage while keeping functionality, balance, proportion and scale in mind," Bernadette notes.

Built on a foundation of white, the rooms are luminous, light and airy. Every element of the design serves a distinct purpose, ensuring that the space feels open, efficient and welcoming.

PAGE 150 A Dutch wooden door keeps the pale pink exterior of the quaint cottage (painted in Impatiens Petal by Sherwin-Williams) from looking too sweet. The top portion can be left open to take advantage of indoor-outdoor living.

PAGE 151 Making the most of the home's small footprint, the kitchen is integrated within the main living space. Against a white backdrop, the cane-backed chairs, bamboo shade/blind and rattan pendant light share a honey tone.

OPPOSITE Bernadette designed, and Andrea created, the space-saving racks to store glasses and drying dishes. Kept handy under the table, ottomans are both stylish and useful as storage and occasional seating.

ABOVE Every design element serves a purpose. Here, vertical space with built-in niches lets utilitarian items become part of the decor.

"Our design ethos revolves around the transformative power of minimalism, where less becomes more and functionality blends seamlessly with style."

Natural materials such as wide-plank pine floors, rattan dining chairs and bamboo shades/blinds complement the white walls for a breezy coastal atmosphere. To add a more intimate touch to the space, Bernadette had vintage family photos printed onto Plexiglass, hence ensuring longevity to the priceless artwork. The synergy between simplicity and elegance demonstrates how a thoughtfully curated blend of design elements can result in the perfect union of style and comfort.

The color scheme was a collaborative decision, including the soft pink exterior hue, which reminds Bernadette of the pastel-painted cottages in Key West. "It has a sense of whimsy while harmonizing with the coastal surroundings." When Pamela and Bernadette were looking at inspirational images together, Pamela expressed her lifelong dream of owning a pink house. "Her heartfelt wish became the guiding inspiration, ensuring that the cottage reflected her individual style."

OPPOSITE Though narrow, a small living room equipped with creature comforts makes maximum use of the space while sustaining the airy design of the main area. Organic materials, rich textures and cohesive hues enrich a neutral palette with streamlined furnishings embracing a fresh, contemporary aesthetic.

BELOW Raising the ceiling revealed the original rafters that contribute to the cottage's history and character. Reconfiguring the layout with new internal walls also provided additional opportunities. Here, a pair of mirrors—of the many installed throughout the house—reflects the entry to one of the bedrooms.

The proximity to the beach played a significant role in inspiring both the interior and the exterior design of Sea La Vie. For the landscaping, Bernadette and Andrea embraced the coastal environment by planting seagrass in the front of the cottage. It's a choice that complements the beachy surroundings and also thrives in the local climate. In an innovative twist, they decided to use beach sand as a ground cover instead of mulch. Bernadette explains: "It not only acts as a moisture barrier for the plants but also supports the biodiversity of the surrounding area."

The outdoor shower and wraparound porch were two existing features of the little house that immediately captured Bernadette's attention.

ABOVE LEFT & RIGHT Though compact, the bathroom offers all modern conveniences. As elsewhere, small plants and cuttings are judiciously incorporated into the design for their fresh and organic presence. Framed black-and-white family photographs enrich the cottage with personality and treasured memories.

Bernadette opted for a pocket door between the bathroom and kitchen. It plays its intended role as well as allowing room for an ample mirror to reflect the kitchen area while magnifying the natural light for an illusion of a larger space.

OPPOSITE & BELOW In keeping with the other interior spaces, the bedrooms share common elements, among which are shapes, textures and finishes that contribute to a relaxed vacation mood. Nightstands/bedside tables, overhead lighting and under-bed storage highlight their charming simplicity and clever functionality.

LEFT & BELOW LEFT Little details make a big impact. Recessed niches display favorite things, while wall space offers a backdrop for old family photos. Hints of pink echo the hue of the cottage exterior.

"While they were already wonderful aspects of the property, we saw an opportunity for a subtle enhancement," she recalls. "Our redesign involved relocating the porch's entry to the front of the building, providing a more inviting approach. Additionally, we sanded and refreshed the outdoor shower, giving it a clean and crisp white finish. These changes not only preserved the charm of the original features but also added a touch of contemporary elegance to the overall design." It's these little details that make the cottage feel like a true beachside oasis and showcase how the environment can inspire and inform the decor choices.

Today, Sea La Vie is a soulful retreat for the warmer months, which provides a serene escape for Pamela and Ara. It is an idyllic haven where they can gather with their friends and family and make new memories.

For a true coastal feel, an outdoor shower is a must. The existing wood was in need of a refresh, so it was sanded down and then a coat of white paint was applied to bring back its clean and crisp appearance.

LEFT Though built in 1997, the cottage has an established appearance thanks in part to its beguiling style boasting a steep roof, covered front entry, dormer windows and Tennessee limestone walls. The picturesque setting, too, evokes that "happily ever after" feeling.

OPPOSITE An original 1800s French pine table and a set of factory stools provide a cozy breakfast spot. The vintage cabinet adds charm while keeping finer dishes safely stored and making them part of the decor.

Storybook Sanctuary

Once upon a time, while traveling through Tennessee, Californians Sarah and Michael McConnell fell under the spell of Leiper's Fork, an enchanting rural village. While exploring the surroundings, the couple came across a tiny cottage, tucked in the woods among rolling hills, which could have easily passed for Goldilocks' hideaway. They were smitten. They bought it and aptly named it Storybook Cottage.

*"Into the forest I go, to lose
my mind and find my soul."*

John Muir

OPPOSITE To maximize the woodland view, Kim skipped curtains and instead mounted fragments from a porch eave to dress up the kitchen window. A lead crystal chandelier adds a graceful note. Open shelving and ironstone serveware are emblematic of country cottages.

RIGHT In lieu of a traditional peg rack, a found branch holds a small chalkboard and fish ornaments with rustic flair.

THERE ARE COTTAGES, and then they are cottages that appear to have come straight from the pages of a fairy-tale book. Quaint, charming and picturesque, they are like no others. They are, well, simply magical. Sarah and Michael could see the potential in this little home, which was structurally in good condition, although the decor was in dire need of a serious makeover. The walls had been covered with layers of paint and parts of the floors were hidden beneath remnants of faded carpet.

To rescue their new home, the couple teamed up with designer and style curator Kim Leggett. Kim's famous City Farmhouse store in Franklin, TN, is a destination for aficionados of one-of-a-kind antiques. As a designer, she is known for weaving together elements with an emotional connection to bring soul to interiors. Her style embraces both sophisticated and simple aesthetics and is inclusive of family heirlooms, upcycled pieces and industrial accents. "Designing a home takes thought if you want to decorate from the heart," says Kim, who has a keen eye for incorporating vintage pieces with meaningful mementos.

It's no surprise that when undertaking to give Sarah and Michael the personal decor they yearned for, Kim listened carefully to their needs and intentionally handpicked furnishings and accessories to surround the couple with things that reflect their life together and bring them joy.

Today, the previously somber, tattered interior, which had walls "the color of a dungeon" according to Kim, has been painted white as snow. The beautiful original poplar planks have been revealed, too, with their distinctive painted diamond pattern of yellow and cream underfoot.

To belie the home's tiny footprint of 800 square feet/74 square meters, Kim opted for furniture that plays double duty in most of the rooms. She carefully edited accessories and included perfectly executed details to create a curated look. Though the overall white palette

and elegant crystal chandeliers convey an ethereal feel, wood tones, touches of blues and yellows, landscape art, souvenirs, photographs and architectural remnants bring the look down to earth, while old books in muted shades add a nostalgic vibe.

Not one space escaped Kim's magic wand. Even the tiny loft, which offers standing room only in the middle, was transformed into fun camp-style sleeping quarters with a pair of twin mattresses laid on the floor and each dressed with vintage camp blankets, as was common practice in the South of days gone by.

ABOVE In the enclosed porch-turned-dining room, new chairs cozy up to a rustic French farm table wearing its original patina. An elegant 1940s chandelier elevates the more rustic materials.

A chandelier draws the eye down from the cathedral ceiling, resulting in a room that feels intimate despite its size. Timeworn objects contribute warmth and texture throughout. Painted poplar flooring shows the passage of time and adds authenticity, while stacks of old books supply an unexpected but fitting decorative touch.

BELOW Minimal window treatments and mostly white furnishings keep the living room awash with light. A collection of 1800s ironstone plates serves up elegant wall decor. The planks' yellow-and-cream diamond pattern is reminiscent of old farmhouse floors.

RIGHT Sculptural wrought-iron candle lanterns flank the ladder-like stairs to the sleeping loft, a favorite spot of visiting children.

OPPOSITE An industrial workshop fan protector provides stylish storage for rag balls of various neutral shades. It plays double duty as a headboard and as a focal point of the room. The industrial bench was salvaged from a sewing factory. A pair of doors has been repurposed into stylish mirrors.

"Crawling into these beds brings back childhood memories of sleeping on 'Baptist pallets,' piles of quilts and blankets used as a makeshift bed when company arrived and decided to stay the night," Kim recalls. "Children always loved those, and it wasn't uncommon to hear ghost stories and giggles from under the covers." The McConnells approve. "There's something so fulfilling about sharing our home with others," says Sarah. "It's the stories Mike and I hear from guests and the memories of the time we shared together that make us smile."

Far from feeling chaotic, the influences from Americana, French and rustic styles mix harmoniously in a unique, personal look that Kim defines as "cottage meets farmhouse. It's not formal or fussy. It's approachable and meaningful." Sarah concurs: "We like clean design that features interesting items and leaves people walking away talking."

"The McConnells gave me complete discretion," Kim says. "Sarah loves interesting conversational elements—unexpected objects incorporated into the design." A large industrial fan cover has become a headboard, while old doors were given a new life as mirrors and objects are displayed on walls in lieu of traditional artwork.

Kim's successful transformation of the cottage stems from her ability to communicate the look that the couple envisioned with authentic pieces that speak of a life well lived yet are perfectly suited for today and tomorrow. "I'm happy to be part of making Sarah and Michael's vision a reality," she says. And so are they.

OPPOSITE A French wheat thresher makes an unexpected canopy in the sleeping loft. Mattresses topped with cushy pillows and vintage wool camp blankets rest on bare floors. A mason jar filled with wildflowers on a worn table has homespun appeal.

ABOVE LEFT & RIGHT Accents of vibrant blue enliven the simplicity of the all-white bathroom. A crystal chandelier infuses subtle touches of romance and luxury. More for shabby style than substance, a small, chippy wall cabinet showcases antique tin salve containers and old medicine bottles.

Floral patterns, uplifting colors and natural textures set the cheerful tone of the Bells' quaint waterside cottage, which was built in the 1920s.

OPPOSITE The vine-draped arbor and quintessential white picket fence extend a warm welcome to guests and bring a smile to those just passing by.

Past Perfect

When Peter Bell explores the shoreline in Barrington, Rhode Island, he keeps a watchful eye out for pieces of seaglass. The colors of these precious souvenirs, popular during the Victorian era, helped define the decor of the diminutive cottage that he and his wife Carey remodeled and decorated.

"A LONG TIME AGO, I saw a pink house in town and right then I knew one day I would have a pink cottage," says Carey. And indeed, she did. With its pale blush exterior, the little home poised by the water brings to mind the delicate hue of frosted seaglass found on walks by the ocean. "I love their many hues," Carey says. "Especially those sea-washed pinks, soft aquas and faded greens."

The couple share a deep affection for little old waterside homes. "This house was built around 1926.

Barrington was a beach community—people used to take the train from Providence to their summer cottages here on the Narragansett Bay," Carey recalls. "In 1938, a hurricane swept most of the quaint houses into the bay, but the fishermen brought them back to shore one by one." She fell in love with this house immediately. "I have always been drawn to small, historic properties, especially ones with original clapboard. They hold so many stories and significance. In most cases, all they need is a second chance."

Whether from the barely covered windows, the floor and table lamps or the chandeliers, the cottage has no shortage of natural or artificial light. Faded, timeworn printed fabrics of various scales and hues play well together in the living room. Enclosing the front porch made room to establish a new dining area.

> "I am excessively fond of a cottage;
> there is always so much comfort,
> so much elegance about them."
>
> Jane Austen

To breathe fresh life into the cottage, the Bells paired their home-improvement talents and fashioned an interior that brims with personality and holds a treasure trove of decorating ideas. "I am lucky that my husband is clever and handy and supports my need to create beautiful tiny spaces. I have the ideas and he executes them," Carey explains. "I am driven by a need to create with pieces that have had a precious life and hold so many memories."

Typical of the homes of the 1920s, the 682-square-foot/63.4-square-meter cottage has an open floor plan reminiscent of the "shotgun houses" of the era. These were named for their linear design—theoretically, a bullet fired through the front entrance could exit the back door without hitting anything. One of the first items on the couple's list was to enclose the front porch to create a dining area. Next, windows were installed on one side of the house to take advantage of the scenic views. Other improvements included remodeling the kitchen and bathroom, installing French doors and creating a patio from discarded bricks. "I wanted to replicate the quaint-looking unleveled sidewalks and streets of the French countryside," Carey explains.

RIGHT Though she favors faded florals, Carey also has an affinity for the signature black-and-white checkerboard pattern on her collection of MacKenzie-Childs homewares. As for furniture, she is known for turning trash into treasures with paint and fabric.

PAGE 178 Lined with a remnant of colorful fabric and protected with clear glass, even a tray doesn't escape the "Carey touch."

PAGE 179 A simple board outfitted with old doorknobs turns a plain wall into a handy place for bags, scarves and coats.

A crown light fixture from Mano a Mano in Bronxville, New York adds a touch of unexpected glamour to the small guest bedroom, which is simply furnished with two iron beds. Not quite a matching pair, both were acquired during separate trips to the famed Brimfield Antique Flea Markets in Massachusetts.

For added charm, the Bells installed an arbor, planted an old-fashioned wisteria vine and an assortment of blooming bushes and built a gate and a picket fence.

Carey is a collector of old treasures, although most of her quests take place farther inland. She combs antiques shops and flea markets for vintage furnishings and castoffs and cottage accessories. Her decorating philosophy, which she describes as "secondhand beach-nik," is approachable and inspiring. "Perfection is not my aim—I like items that are broken, chipped and crooked; anything with an equal dose of patina and purpose," she says. "But nothing too fragile that it couldn't be used and enjoyed." Like an artist, she brings rooms to life with the right balance of color, pattern, texture and whimsy.

Despite the cottage's small footprint, Carey has managed to create a cozy and inviting interior with a flowing aesthetic. "My goal was to create soothing yet lively spaces," she says.

ABOVE LEFT, ABOVE RIGHT & LEFT The bed practically fills the main bedroom, but barely-there curtains and soft-hued bedding merge to make it feel cozy, not cramped. Displayed on a tray, jewelry becomes part of the decor. An apothecary cabinet delivers a wealth of storage and even provides a narrow display area in the teeny bathroom.

RIGHT A rescued cabinet, treated to a glossy coat of salmon pink, adds much needed kitchen storage, while the exposed shelving offers ample display space for collected enamelware. Floral wallpaper pulls the colors together and contributes to the charm of the hard-working room.

OPPOSITE To take advantage of its waterside location and extend the cottage's small footprint, the Bells added a brick patio framed with a picket fence. They furnished it with rescued and refinished wicker furniture, along with comfy pillows and cushions that Carey made using remnants of vintage floral fabric.

She began with a white backdrop to act as an anchor for floral chintz window panels, slipcovers and pillows. Black-checked accents can also be found throughout.

"My furniture is 95%secondhand—I don't believe I will ever be tempted to buy new," says Carey. "It's like mixing diamonds and rhinestones." One piece might have six layers of colored paints depending on her mood. "I have an affinity for painted pieces and have been known to buy them just for the color," she says. "That applies equally to vintage fabrics, especially those with texture or pattern. My couches and chairs always sport comfy slipcovers that I have made myself."

Each room also features repurposed accessories, such as an old plank Peter made into a peg rack by adding doorknobs, a silk scarf Carey framed as art—which took more than 400 pins to hold it in place—or an old window reborn as a tray. The couple see endless possibilities around them. "We take ordinary items and spaces and make them unique and personal," Carey says.

Thanks to Carey and Peter's appreciation for the past, the once unassuming little cottage has reached its full potential. They have embraced the charm of its era, its picturesque surroundings and its unique personality with comfort and elegance.

Sources

US FLEA MARKETS

Remember, when it comes to flea markets, you should arrive early—first come, first served!

Barnhouse Vintage Market
Various locations, CA
www.barnhousevintagemarket.com

Big Chicken Barn
Ellsworth, ME
www.bigchickenbarn.com

Brimfield Antique & Flea Markets
Brimfield, MA
www.brimfieldantiquefleamarket.com

The Fancy Flea
Various locations, FL
www.fancyflea.net

The Fleur de Flea
Louisville, KY
www.thefleurdeflea.com

Funky Flea Market
Fayetteville, AR
www.funkynwa.com

Goat Hill Fair
Watsonville, CA
www.goathillfair.com

Junk Bonanza
Shakopee, MN
junkbonanza.com

Long Beach Antique Market
Long Beach, CA
www.longbeachantiquemarket.com

Petaluma Antique Faire
Petaluma, CA
www.petalumadowntown.com/
    antique-show

Rose Bowl Flea Market
Pasadena, CA
www.rgcshow.com

Round Top and Warrenton Antique Shows
Round Top and Warrenton, TX
www.antiqueweekend.com

Santa Monica Antique and Vintage Market
Santa Monica, CA
www.santamonicaairport
    antiquemarket.com

Sweet Salvage
Phoenix, AZ
www.sweetsalvage.net

US SHOPS

Blu Canoe
Newport Beach, CA
www.theblucanoe.com

City Farmhouse
Franklin, TN
www.cityfarmhousefranklin.com

The Consignment Gallery
Bedford, NH
www.consignmentgallery.com

Dobbin St. Vintage Co-Op
Brooklyn, NY
www.dobbinstcoop.com

Double Take
Santa Fe, NM
www.santafedoubletake.com

Mongers Market
Bridgeport, CT
www.mongers-market.com

New Americana Home
Denver, CO
newamericanahome.com

Newburgh Vintage Emporium
Newburgh, NY
www.newburghvintage
    emporium.com

Oddballs Nifty Thrift
Fort Lauderdale, FL
www.facebook.com/
OddballsNiftyThrift

Pathway Market
Grand Rapids, MI
www.pathwaymarketgr.com

Posh
Venice, FL
www.poshonpalm.com

Sarasota Architectural Salvage,
Sarasota, FL
www.sarasotasalvage.com

South Side Vintage
Minneapolis, MN
www.southsidevintage.com

Summer Cottage Antiques
Petaluma, CA
www.summercottageantiques.com

Tumbleweed & Dandelion
Venice, CA
www.tumbleweedanddandelion.com

Urban Suburban Antiques
Birmingham, AL
www.facebook.com/
    urbansuburbanantiques

Valerie's Vintage & Supply Co
Santa Ynez, CA
valeriesvintageandsupply.com

Vignettes
San Diego, CA
www.vignettesdecor.com

UK MARKETS

The Decorative Fair
Battersea Park, London
ww.decorativefair.com

The Great Wetherby Racecourse Antiques and Collectors Fair
Wetherby, West Yorkshire
www.jaguarfairs.com/wetherby

International Antique and Collectors Fair
Various locations, nationwide
www.iacf.co.uk

Malvern Flea & Collectors Fair
Malvern, Worcestershire
www.b2bfairs.co.uk

Sunbury Antiques Market
Sunbury-on-Thames, Surrey
www.sunburyantiques.com

UK SHOPS

Alfies Antique Market
Marylebone, London
www.alfiesantiques.com

Lorfords Antiques
Tetbury, Gloucestershire
www.lorfordsantiques.com

The Old Cinema
Chiswick, London
www.theoldcinema.co.uk

RE
Corbridge, Northumberland
www.re-foundobjects.com

Scaramanga
Cupar, Fife
www.scaramangashop.co.uk

ONLINE

1stDIBS
www.1stdibs.com

Chairish
www.chairish.com

eBay
www.ebay.com
www.ebay.co.uk

Etsy
www.etsy.com

Hoarde Vintage
www.thehoarde.com

One Kings Lane
www.onekingslane.com/c/
    shop-vintage

Popuphome
www.popuphome.com

Rachel Ashwell Shabby Chic
www.shabbychic.com

Rejuvenation
www.rejuvenation.com/shop/vintage

Revival Rugs
www.revivalrugs.com

Selling Antiques
www.sellingantiques.co.uk

Tat London
www.tat-london.co.uk

Picture Credits

All photography by Mark Lohman unless otherwise stated. All photography copyright © CICO Books 2024 unless otherwise stated.

Key: Ph = photographer; a = above; b = below; l = left; c = center; r = right.

Page 1 The Florida home of designer Susie Holt of Posh, IG @susie.holt www.poshonpalm.com; 2 The home of Cathy and Jeff Collins in Arkansas; 3 The Florida home of designer Susie Holt of Posh, IG @susie.holt www.poshonpalm.com; 4 The home of Carey Bell in Rhode Island; 5 a The home of Kate Keesee in California, IG @katekeeseeoc; 5 c & b The home of Donna Morgan in California; 7 The Florida home of designer Susie Holt of Posh, IG @susie.holt www.poshonpalm.com; 8–9 Ph © John Ellis/The home of Louise O'Brien-Schridde and Daniel Schridde in California, www.obrienschriddedesigns.com; 10 The home of Cathy and Jeff Collins in Arkansas; 11 a Ph © John Ellis/The home of Louise O'Brien-Schridde and Daniel Schridde in California, www.obrienschriddedesigns.com; 11 c The home of Cathy and Jeff Collins in Arkansas; 11 b Ph © Edmund Barr/The home of Sarah and Michael McConnell in Leiper's Fork, Tennessee, designed by Kim Leggett of City Farmhouse, www.cityfarmhousefranklin.com; 12 a The home of Donna Morgan in California; 12 bl The home of Kate Keesee in California, IG @katekeeseeoc; 12 br The home of Annie and Darryl McCreary in Tennessee, with styling by Jenn Palmer; 13 The home of Kate Keesee in California, IG @katekeeseeoc; 14 Ph © John Ellis/The home of Louise O'Brien-Schridde and Daniel Schridde in California, www.obrienschriddedesigns.com; 15 The home of Donna Morgan in California; 16 l & r Ph © Andrea Pietrangeli/The home of Pamela and Ara Millette in Rhode Island, designed by Bernadette Heydt, www.heydthome.com; 17 Ph © Edmund Barr/The home of Sarah and Michael McConnell in Leiper's Fork, Tennessee, designed by Kim Leggett of City Farmhouse, www.cityfarmhousefranklin.com; 18 Ph © Andrea Pietrangeli/The home of Pamela and Ara Millette in Rhode Island, designed by Bernadette Heydt, www.heydthome.com 19 l & r The home of jewelry designer Laurie Lenfestey of Bittersweet Designs in New Mexico, www.bittersweetdesigns.com; 20 The home of Carlos Pagel and Carl Morton in upstate New York; 21 l The home of Kate Keesee in California, IG @katekeeseeoc; 21 r Ph © Edmund Barr/The home of Sarah and Michael McConnell in Leiper's Fork, Tennessee, designed by Kim Leggett of City Farmhouse, www.cityfarmhousefranklin.com; 22 & 23 a The home of Donna Morgan in California; 23 c The home of Cathy and Jeff Collins in Arkansas; 23 b The home of author Fifi O'Neill in Florida; 24 The home of Annie and Darryl McCreary in Tennessee, with styling by Jenn Palmer; 25 a The home of Carey Bell in Rhode Island; 25 b The home of jewelry designer Laurie Lenfestey of Bittersweet Designs in New Mexico, www.bittersweetdesigns.com; 26 a & c Ph © John Ellis/The home of Louise O'Brien-Schridde and Daniel Schridde in California, www.obrienschriddedesigns.com; 26 b The home of Donna Morgan in California; 27 The home of textile artist Carol Riley in Rhode Island, IG @tattershandmadeclothing; 28 The home of Cathy and Jeff Collins in Arkansas; 29 The home of Donna Morgan in California; 30 The home of Carey Bell in Rhode Island; 31 a Ph © Andrea Pietrangeli/The home of Pamela and Ara Millette in Rhode Island, designed by Bernadette Heydt, www.heydthome.com 31 b The home of Kate Keesee in California, IG @katekeeseeoc; 32 l The home of author Fifi O'Neill in Florida; 32 ar The home of jewelry designer Laurie Lenfestey of Bittersweet Designs in New Mexico, www.bittersweetdesigns.com; 32 br & 33 The Florida home of designer Susie Holt of Posh, IG @susie.holt www.poshonpalm.com; 34 Ph © John Ellis/The home of Louise O'Brien-Schridde and Daniel Schridde in California, www.obrienschriddedesigns.com; 35 The home of Carey Bell in Rhode Island; 36 The home of Donna Morgan in California; 37 a Ph © Andrea Pietrangeli/The home of Pamela and Ara Millette in Rhode Island, designed by Bernadette Heydt, www.heydthome.com; 37 bl The home of Donna Morgan in California; 37 br Ph © Andrea Pietrangeli/The home of Pamela and Ara Millette in Rhode Island, designed by Bernadette Heydt, www.heydthome.com; 38–51 Ph © John Ellis/The home of Louise O'Brien-Schridde and Daniel Schridde in California, www.obrienschriddedesigns.com; 52–61 The home of Cathy and Jeff Collins in Arkansas; 62–73 The home of author Fifi O'Neill in Florida; 74–85 The home of Carlos Pagel and Carl Morton in upstate New York; 86–95 The Florida home of designer Susie Holt of Posh, IG @susie.holt www.poshonpalm.com; 96–105 The home of jewelry designer Laurie Lenfestey of Bittersweet Designs in New Mexico, www.bittersweetdesigns.com; 106–117 The home of textile artist Carol Riley in Rhode Island, IG @tattershandmadeclothing; 118–127 The home of Donna Morgan in California; 128–137 The home of Kate Keesee in California, IG @katekeeseeoc; 138–149 The home of Annie and Darryl McCreary in Tennessee, with styling by Jenn Palmer; 150–161 Ph © Andrea Pietrangeli/The home of Pamela and Ara Millette in Rhode Island, designed by Bernadette Heydt, www.heydthome.com; 162–171 Ph © Edmund Barr/The home of Sarah and Michael McConnell in Leiper's Fork, Tennessee, designed by Kim Leggett of City Farmhouse, www.cityfarmhousefranklin.com; 172–183 The home of Carey Bell in Rhode Island; 184 The home of Carey Bell in Rhode Island; 185 Ph © Edmund Barr/The home of Sarah and Michael McConnell in Leiper's Fork, Tennessee, designed by Kim Leggett of City Farmhouse, www.cityfarmhousefranklin.com; 187 The Florida home of designer Susie Holt of Posh, IG @susie.holt www.poshonpalm.com; 188 The home of Annie and Darryl McCreary in Tennessee, with styling by Jenn Palmer; 192 The home of Cathy and Jeff Collins in Arkansas; Front cover The home of author Fifi O'Neill in Florida; Back cover The Florida home of designer Susie Holt of Posh, IG @susie.holt www.poshonpalm.com; Endpapers Ph © John Ellis/The home of Louise O'Brien-Schridde and Daniel Schridde in California, www.obrienschriddedesigns.com.

Business Credits

Key: a = above; b = below; l = left; c = center; r = right.

Bernadette Heydt
Interior designer
Heydt Home
11 Bowler Lane
Newport, RI 02840
401-426-1883
www.heydthome.com
IG: @heydt_home
Pages 16 l, 16 r, 18, 31 a, 37 a, 37 br, 150—161.

Susie Holt
Designer
IG: @susie.holt
Posh
327 W Venice Ave
Venice, FL 34285
941-786-1008
www.poshonpalm.com
Pages 1, 3, 7, 32 br, 33, 86—95, 187.

Kate Keesee
Design and DIY
IG: @katekeeseeoc
Pages 5 a, 12 bl, 13, 21 l, 31 b, 128—137.

Kim Leggett
Antiques and interior design
City Farmhouse
117 3rd Ave N
Franklin, TN 37064
615-268-0216
www.cityhousefranklin.com
IG: @cityfarmhouse
Pages 11 b, 17, 21 r, 162—171, 185.

Laurie Lenfestey
Jewelry designer
IG: @bittersweetdesignslaurie

Bittersweet Designs
667 Canyon Road
Santa Fe, NM 87501
505-988-8006
www.bittersweetdesigns.com
Pages 19 l, 19 r, 25 b, 32 ar, 96—105.

Annie McCreary
Seamstress
My Swallow's Nest
www.myswallowsnest.net
IG: @myswallowsnest
Pages 12 br, 24, 138—149, 188.

Donna Morgan
Artist and home designer
interiorlove08@gmail.com
Pages 5 c, 5 b, 12 a, 15, 22, 23 a, 26 b, 29, 36, 37 bl, 118—127.

Carol Riley
Textile artist
Tatters Handmade Clothing
324 Main Street
Warren, RI 02885
tatters-the-church-palace.square.site
IG: @tattershandmadeclothing
Pages 27, 106—117.

Louise O'Brien-Schridde and Daniel Schridde
Landscape designers
O'Brien Schridde Designs
911 North Evergreen Street
Burbank, CA 91505
818-281-9256
www.obrienschriddedesigns.com
Pages 8—9, 11 a, 14, 26 a, 26 c, 34, 38—51, endpapers.

Index

Page numbers in *italic* refer to the illustrations

Acknowledgments

One might think that after working with the same publisher for 15 years, thanking all the people involved in the process of creating a book might feel repetitious. On the contrary, every time I get to this last part, I am filled with gratitude for everyone at CICO Books for trusting that I will come up with the right homes and the right words. Having that kind of support is a rare occurrence these days.

My heartfelt thanks to David Peters, Annabel Morgan, Leslie Harrington, Sally Powell, Toni Kay, Sophie Devlin and Gordana Simakovic for all you do. I think of you as my British family and whatever the future brings, you will always be in my heart.

The Soulful Cottage is special because all the homes hold much more than the sum of their parts. They mirror their owners' stories, their bond with their families, their souls. Each home and each room, inspires by its meaningful contents.

It is said that "A picture is worth a thousand words", and the photography of my main co-conspirator, Mark Lohman proves the point. Thank you, Mark.

Carey and Peter Bell, Cathy and Jeff Collins, Mark and Susie Holt, Kate Keesee, Laurie Lenfestey, Sarah and Michael McConnell, Pamela and Ara Millette, Annie and Darryl McCreary, Donna Morgan, Carl Morton, and Carlos Pagel, Carol and Mike Riley, and Daniel and Louise Schridde, thank you for letting us photograph your homes and sharing your precious memories with all of us. Writing your stories has brought me much comfort. My wish is that it will do the same for you and for anyone looking for inspiration, comfort and that much needed sense of humanity and belonging.

With love, always,
Fifi